FOOTBALL
for the Utterly
CONFUSED

TOM FLORES
and BOB O'CONNOR

New York Chicago San Francisco Lisbon London Madrid Mexico City
Milan New Delhi San Juan Seoul Singapore Sydney Toronto

Library of Congress Cataloging-in-Publication Data

Flores, Tom.
     Football for the utterly confused / by Tom Flores and Bob O'Connor.
         p.   cm.
     ISBN-13: 978-0-07-162858-7 (alk. paper)
     ISBN-10: 0-07-162858-4
     1. Football.   I. O'Connor, Robert, 1932–   II. Title.

  GV951.O35   2009
  796.332—dc22   2009013543

To Tyler Wells—just graduating from the flag football leagues to the tackle game. We know you will enjoy playing this very special game.

1 2 3 4 5 6 7 8 9 10 11 12 13 14 15 16 17 18 19 20 21 22 FGR/FGR 0 9

ISBN 978-0-07-162858-7
MHID   0-07-162858-4

McGraw-Hill books are available at special quantity discounts to use as premiums and sales promotions, or for use in corporate training programs. To contact a representative please e-mail us at bulksales@mcgraw-hill.com.

This book is printed on acid-free paper.

Contents

PART I   AN INTRODUCTION TO THE GAMES OF FOOTBALL

Chapter 1   American Football Is a Very Different Kind of Game   3

Chapter 2   The Game in Our Society   23

PART II   THE WHYS AND HOWS OF THE Xs AND Os

Chapter 3   A Philosophy of Coaching and Playing   33

Chapter 4   Theories of Winning   43

Chapter 5   Theories of Offensive Formations   51

Chapter 6   The Running Attack   57

Chapter 7   Passing Theory   61

Chapter 8   Defensive Theory   69

Chapter 9   Kicking Game Theory   81

PART III   A COACH'S IDEA OF THE GAME: BEYOND THE Xs AND Os

Chapter 10   Strategy: Deciding on the Game Plan   95

Chapter 11   Tactics: Making Adjustments During the Game   109

Chapter 12   Making the Big Plays and Converting Third Downs   115

Chapter 13   Scoring in the Scoring Zones   123

Chapter 14   Penalties and Turnovers—the Viruses That Can Kill You   127

Chapter 15   Handling the Clock   137

PART IV   ENJOYING THE GAMES OF FOOTBALL

Chapter 16   How to Watch a Game   147

Chapter 17   Playing and Coaching Flag and Touch Football   153

Chapter 18   Coaching Youth Football   165

Chapter 19   Playing Fantasy Football   173

Epilogue   185

Glossary of Common Football Terms   187

Index   195

DID YOU KNOW

- There are more than 200 rule differences between college and professional football.

- There are more than 200 more differences between college and high school rules.

- John Wayne, the film immortal, starred at the University of Southern California under the name "Duke" Morrison.

- TV actor Mark Harmon starred at UCLA at quarterback. His father, Tom, won the Heisman Trophy as the best college football player of 1940.

- There are more varied styles of play at the high school level than the college level and more variations at the college level than at the professional level.

- While American football uses 11 players, Canadian football uses 12.

- The stimulating effects of the halftime "pep talk," which is supposed to charge up the players for the next half, last about 5 to 10 minutes. The pep talk makes a great movie scene but isn't all that effective in changing the outcome of the game.

PART I

An Introduction to the Games of Football

CHAPTER 1

American Football Is a Very Different Kind of Game

There are the games that flow, like hockey and soccer. There are games that stop periodically so that new tactics can be instituted. Basketball could fit in either category, since time-outs give the coach a few seconds to change offensive or defensive tactics. Boxing stops every three minutes so the athlete can rest and the manager can suggest changes in how to attack.

Then there are games that stop often, allowing the athlete, the players, or the coach to make changes in tactics depending on the score or the game situation. Golf stops after every shot and a new situation has arrived, so the golfer must make several decisions before making the next shot. How far is the hole? Is the wind a factor? Is the ball lying on the fairway with short grass? Which club does the shot require? Should a longer club be used but hit more easily for better control? A chess player will also have some time to consider the next move—and several possible moves in advance. Then there's football.

The Complex Game

The American brand of football has far more variables than golf or chess. After every five-second play there will be nearly a minute for the referee to put the ball at the proper spot, for the players to huddle, and for the play-caller to determine the next play. As in chess, the play will often be a step in a progression of plays with a definite objective. As in golf, the weather, the position of the ball, and the score will all be considered. But in football, a number of other factors enter the mix. Injuries to players on either team will need to be addressed. Were the injuries known before the game, or did they occur during the game? How well has each coach prepared for the game? How motivated are the players to win? How effectively does each coach handle the changing game situations?

Because of the nearly infinite number of possibilities that can occur during a game, football coaches will have "scouted" the opponent to find out what the team is likely to do in many situations. What plays are likely to come from each offensive formation it uses? What are the opposing players likely to do in each part of the field? Do they limit their offense when they are near the goal they are defending? Do they run to their right more often than to their left?

How long does it take the team's punter to kick the ball? Any more than a total time of 2.2 seconds increases the defense's chance of blocking the punt, and a blocked punt is equivalent to an offensive play of 40 to 80 yards.

Based on the scouting analyses, the coach determines a "game plan." One of the key elements of a game plan is deciding how to exploit mismatches. Is there an offensive lineman who can overpower the defensive lineman opposite him? If so the coach might plan on running over his area when yardage is needed. How can a team get its fastest pass receiver on the other team's slowest defender? If the defense generally employs a zone defense, perhaps lining up the best receiver in a special spot, like in a slot, would deliver a mismatch. If the opponent plays a man-to-man defense, maybe the offensive team can run two or three receivers in crossing routes, perhaps getting a defender slowed up as the defenders and offensive players are crossing. Maybe the offense can run a screen pass, throwing to the best receiver behind the line of scrimmage. If the opponents have a great defensive lineman, what various blocking patterns can be used to control his pass rush?

Line of scrimmage: An area approximately a foot wide (the width of the ball) that stretches from sideline to sideline.

Screen: A pass behind the line of scrimmage after a deep drop by the quarterback. Some linemen pull to lead the receiver.

Football has been called a violent chess match. It is the thinking part of the game that fascinates so many of the coaches and players, but the thinking involves more than just the team strategy. Every individual player has his own battle. For the offensive and defensive linemen it is a one-against-one battle on every play. Football is more than a jousting match. There are team strategies and tactics and individual techniques and countertechniques that only experienced coaches understand completely. Understanding some of these will make you a more astute spectator.

What to Watch For

Let's say the offensive lineman takes a step back and sets up to block. This signals the defensive lineman that it is a pass or a fake pass, such as a draw play. He then charges the offensive lineman. The offensive player punches the defender in the chest with both hands, his palms open. The defender must charge and use one of several pass rush techniques that he has practiced for months:

- If he sees that the offensive player has his weight back, he might try a "bull rush" and run over him.

- If he senses that the offensive player has too much weight forward, he can grab the blocker's arms or shoulder pads, pull him forward, then run past him to the passer.

- If the blocker is balanced, the pass rusher will choose a side to rush. To do this he must either take away one of the blocker's hands by grabbing one or knock him off balance by hitting him hard on the shoulder. This is called a club. Once the blocker is off balance, the defender can charge to a side, usually by using a "swim" move with the arm that was not used in the club or the grab. So if the defender clubbed the left shoulder of the blocker with his right arm, his left arm would swim over the left shoulder of the blocker.

- If the blocker is short, this swim move might work. If the blocker is taller, the rusher can rip his left arm under the left shoulder of the blocker and duck under the shoulder as he charges.

These are only a few of the moves the defender can use. There are also countermoves the blocker can use for every pass rush move of the defender.

Counter: A play that ends going a different direction than the initial flow of the backs would indicate.

Draw: A fake pass that ends with one of the backs carrying the ball after the defensive linemen are drawn in on the pass rush.

Each player works on his own skills, but none of the players understand the whole picture until they study the game in depth. Many fans who have learned the game with a TV clicker in one hand and a beer in the other think they understand the game. What they understand is part of the tactics of the games they watch. But they haven't had access to the 100-page scouting reports and the weeklong coaches' meetings that have taken into consideration what the other team has done against their team the last few years, what it has done against other teams this year, and the injuries of each team and how they may impact the game, along with where individual or team mismatches can be employed.

The History of the Game

When you look at a history, the question is how far back to go. We can start with the first college football game in 1869, or we can go all the way back to the Han dynasty in China 2,200 years ago to find *tsu tsu*, a game where the ball was kicked. Or we can limit the search to Europe and America and start 1,500 years ago with an Italian game called *harpastum*. We don't know if this was only a kicking game or if the players could use their hands. (Since Italians have a reputation for talking with their hands, it is doubtful that they would invent a game where they couldn't talk—or use their hands!) The mayhem that resulted caused more than a few injuries. The Italians brought the game to England, probably during the Roman occupation. The roughness was also evident in the English game, so King Henry II banned it about A.D. 1200, saying that it interfered with the sport of archery, which was essential to national defense. The game never really died, and 400 years later King James allowed the game to be played legally again.

Then in the 1500s the Italians came up with another game. *Calcio* was played with 27 players on each team, and they were allowed to kick, pass, or carry the ball over the goal line.

Meanwhile, back in jolly old England, by 1580 soccer was being played in the upper-class schools such as Cambridge. Soon the various colleges were arranging games between themselves. This required that formal rules be developed. There was some conflict over whether use of the hands should be allowed or not. But it was soon settled that only the goalkeeper could use his hands. Then tradition tells us that at Rugby School in 1823 a young lad, William Webb Ellis, was not content to just kick the ball, so he picked it up and ran with it. His classmates liked the idea of running with the ball, so they formulated new rules for the new game—rugby. It wasn't until 1845 that the first formal rugby rules were written. If you have seen rugby in America, you probably saw the "rugby union" game with its scrums, lateral passing, punting on the run, and placekicks.

As with any new game there were changes in the early years. In 1877 the number of players was reduced from 20 to 15. Under the early rules, running the ball over the goal line did not score a point, it merely entitled the team to "try" a kick that would actually score a point. Running the ball over the goal line is still called a try. The scoring of a try, running the ball over the goal line, gradually increased from no points to five points by 1992.

Historically Speaking

Rugby was first played with a round leather ball inflated with pig's bladder. That, of course, is the reason that an American football, made of cowhide, is called a pigskin. When the rubber bladder was perfected it became possible to change the shape of the ball to an oval that was more easily carried.

Our American game kept elements of the rugby union scrum. But we kept only five to seven blockers in one line, while the rugby union scrum had eight in two lines. Rugby has enjoyed some popularity in the United States. In fact the United States won the 1920 Olympic rugby championship. When Teddy Roosevelt charged that football was causing too many injuries, rugby teams replaced many high school football teams. As a high school and college sport played in the winter or spring, many football players continue their interest in the other pigskin game.

In the 1800s, attempts were made to standardize rules for both rugby and soccer. Prior to this the rules for each game were generally determined by the two teams before the game, both in England and in the United States. The first official college games played in North America were quite different from one another. The first recorded intercollegiate game was in 1869 between Rutgers and Princeton. Each team had 25 players. Since Rutgers was the home team, they used their rules. The teams were not allowed to carry or throw the ball. A point was scored if a player kicked the ball into the opponent's goal. The first team to score six points won. Rutgers won 6–4. In a rematch a week later using Princeton's rules, Princeton won 8–0.

The next year Columbia joined, then Yale and some other local colleges. In 1873 the schools decided that they needed a standard set of rules if they were going to play each other often. The rules chosen resembled those of soccer.

Meanwhile, in Massachusetts, Harvard was playing a rather different game. The scholars of Harvard played a game that allowed the ball to be carried. Called the "Boston game," it was more like rugby. The Harvard players weren't interested in the soccer-style game of the colleges to the south, and they refused to attend the "rules" meeting. Then in 1874 McGill University of Montreal ventured to Harvard for a pair of games. Harvard won the first 3–0 using the Harvard rules. The next day they played using the rugby rules of McGill, and neither team scored. The teams decided that they liked the idea of awarding points when a player crossed the goal line and touched the ball down. They also gave a point for the kicking try after the touchdown. Rugby rules still did not give points for running the ball over the goal line.

Early Rules

The development of formal rules for football and rugby made the games more civil than the older mob-style games that in earlier Europe had pitted town against town and in American universities class against class, like the annual "Bloody Monday" game that pitted the Harvard freshmen against the sophomores. Often these were keep-away-like games where teenage enthusiasm and the common lack of common sense led to large numbers of injuries— commonly serious, often deadly. In the early 1860s, this usually led to a college or city prohibiting these mass games. But what young man can sit quietly studying when there is a ball and some willing lads ready to do mock battle in whatever guise is available? The teams had to be reduced from battalion size to platoon size, and some rules had to be introduced. Still, boys being boys, and not having the sense of their sisters, ferocity trumped friendliness and the mayhem just continued with smaller teams.

In 1875 Harvard played Yale under some modified rules that allowed carrying the ball. Yale lost 4–0 but liked the idea of carrying the ball. Some players from Princeton saw the game and liked it as well, so they brought it back home. The next year players from Harvard, Princeton, Columbia, and Yale met in Springfield, Massachusetts, to formulate rules for this new game. College football expanded from 8 teams in 1880 to 43 in 1900, and there are more than 600 NCAA schools today.

Springfield deserves a special place in American sport. Basketball and volleyball were invented there, and it is also where the first rules of American football were drawn up. As you can see, American football has evolved from the ball-carrying game of rugby, but the official rules of the two games were developed only four years apart.

But even with the new rules, the game was very rough. Mass formations developed where the offensive teammates would lock arms and run over the defenders while protecting the ballcarrier inside the "flying wedge." The excessive roughness and the 18 fatalities in 1905 led President Teddy Roosevelt to threaten to ban the sport. So in December of 1905, a group of 62 colleges met in New York to make rules that would make the game less lethal. The forward pass was allowed. Prior to this time only the rugby-type lateral pass had been allowed. The forerunner of the NCAA, the overseer of college sport, was also instituted at this meeting.

 Lateral pass: A pass thrown parallel with the line of scrimmage or backward. It can be thrown overhand or underhand.

From the beginning, Walter Camp, called the father of American football, was the major influence on American football rules. He was a multisport athlete at Yale. As an underclassman he was one of the representatives at the Springfield meeting. One of the early changes to the game was dropping the number of players from 15 to 13 and finally to 11 in 1880. Yale had played an English team from Eton that played 11-man rugby. They liked the game and pressured the other teams to adopt the change. Playing with 11 men put more emphasis on speed and less on pure strength.

Camp was instrumental in changing the rugby scrum to a line of scrimmage. Rugby scrums, with eight men on each side, tried to push each other past the ball so that the successful team's backs could pick up the ball and run with it. Camp's idea was to give the ball to one team and give it three tries to make five yards. If it made the five yards it got three more downs. In 1906 the rule was changed to three downs to gain 10 yards. Then in 1912 it was changed to four downs to go 10 yards. Tackling below the waist, not permitted in rugby, was allowed.

While the forward pass was allowed, with the large rugby-type ball it was very difficult to throw. Then, because the essence of football is running, Camp and his friends required that the passer had to be at least 5 yards deep and 5 yards wider than the snapper, and an incomplete pass was penalized 15 yards. Then in 1910 it became illegal to throw the ball more than 20 yards because the pass was taking away from the real game of football. In 1931 the shape of the ball was changed to make it easier to pass. Then in 1934 the five-yard penalty for a second incomplete pass in a series was eliminated. In 1941 the rule requiring a pass incomplete in the end zone to go to the other team as a touchback was rescinded. Then in 1945 the passer was allowed to throw from anywhere behind the line of scrimmage.

Touchback: A play that ends behind the receiver's goal line but in which the impetus of the ball was generated by the other team. There is no score. The ball is moved to the 20-yard line for the first down.

Every year another 5 to 10 rules are added. For college football, they are based largely on the recommendations of the American Football Coaches Association. In 2008, college football added 17 new rules, several related to aiding the game officials to review their decisions by way of instant video replay. The high school rules increased by seven, and the NFL rules increased by eight. Generally these rules have to do with speeding up the game or making it safer. The rule books are about a quarter-inch thick and in small print. There is also a companion book that gives rule interpretations for varying situations. Football is definitely a complicated game—the world's most complicated game.

The Development of Theory

Since the game stopped after every runner was "downed," it gave coaches and players a chance to change tactics after every play. A second down with eight yards to go is certainly a different situation than a second down with one yard to go.

Sport historians tell us that the British played their games according to the spirit of the rules. Americans are more likely to look for loopholes in a rule. Coaches are often like California lawyers, bending the rules in order to win. Knute Rockne of Notre Dame developed a shift where the players lined up in a T formation and on the signal jumped to a new position—right or left. The center would snap the ball just as the back's feet landed in the new position. The precision of the shift was done to a four count. The ball was snapped on the fourth count. The defense didn't have a chance to adjust to the new formation. The way Notre Dame shifted was legal, but it seemed to give too much of an advantage to the offense, so the rules committee made the rule that after a shift all players must remain stationary for a full second. Another coach had leather football cutouts sewed to the uniforms so that the defense would have a hard time figuring out who had the ball—so a new rule was called for!

Snap: The act of putting the ball in play. It can be handed to the quarterback or thrown (between the legs or to the side) to a back.

Snapper: The offensive lineman who puts the ball in play, usually the center.

Others looked for advantages within the spirit of the rules. Amos Alonzo Stagg was a divinity student at Yale and played there for four years. He was an end on the first All-American team. He then went to Springfield College for a graduate degree. Springfield was about to field its first football team. Being a student, Stagg could still play on the team. The coach was James Naismith, who had just invented the game of basketball. Naismith decided to devote his time to developing basketball, so he stepped down as football coach, and Stagg took the reins. Stagg then went to the University of Chicago, where he coached football, baseball, basketball, and track. He retired at 70 and took a job at College of the Pacific, the alma mater of one of this book's authors. He coached until he was 100 years old and died at 103. Stagg was the first to use numbers on the jerseys and the first to use a huddle, and he invented the shift that Rockne perfected. He invented a number of plays as well, including the double reverse and the "statue of liberty" play. He also first used the man in motion—having one man moving laterally or backward when the ball is snapped.

With the new rules of 1905 and 1906, passing became more important. Coach Eddie Cochems of St. Louis University designed the first pass play in 1906. The pass was looked down upon in the East as being part of a weak or inferior style of play, so it was left to the South and the Midwest to explore its potential. And its potential is much greater when a defense is set to stop running plays.

Historically Speaking Notre Dame tailback Gus Dorais and end Knute Rockne practiced passing all summer when working at Cedar Point in Ohio in 1913. Then in the fall they used the pass to trounce a heavily favored Army team 35 to 13 and establish Notre Dame as a national power. Rockne had to choose between taking a job at Notre Dame as a chemistry professor and being its football coach. His decision made Notre Dame the premier team in the country. He left a record of 105–12–5 when his life was prematurely claimed in 1931 in an airplane crash.

As the passing game developed, new formations and new theories emerged. For example, perhaps you have seen the revolutionary "bunch" formation where a split end and two backs are set wide and close together. From this set the backs can run crossing patterns that will confuse the defensive backs. That same formation was used 100 years ago by the University of Idaho. Then there is the shotgun or spread formation where the quarterback, the passer, sets himself three or four yards back from his normal position directly behind the center. That was used by Coach Jim Phelan at St. Mary's in the 1940s and by Red Sanders at UCLA in the 1950s when he split the ends and wingback in his single wing formation. The shotgun goes even further back, as a number of teams used such formations in the early 1900s.

Shotgun: A formation in which the quarterback sets several yards behind the center to be able to see the field better on a pass play. More wide receivers are also used.

Changes in the Game

Coaches developed novel offenses, then later more effective defenses, while running backs dazzled the spectators. In the mid-1920s Red Grange, the Galloping Ghost, led Illinois to glory while the Four Horsemen trampled the foes of Notre Dame. Around the time of World War I, Pop Warner developed the single and double wing formations and Rockne perfected the shift at Notre Dame. The single wing had a back, a wingback, playing a yard outside an end. The double wing had wingbacks outside of each end.

In 1940 Clark Shaughnessy popularized the T formation with a man in motion while at Stanford. This was probably the most important innovation for modern college and pro football. Sid Gilman and Bill Walsh modernized and perfected the passing game, and it became an equal or even superior partner to the run. Quarterbacks now dominate the Heisman Trophy winners and the pro Most Valuable Player awards.

In order to be able to attack the whole width of the field, teams began to put one, two, or three receivers wide—wide enough that they could catch quick passes near the sidelines, go deep, or make quick slanting patterns to the inside. Defensive teams had to stop the long passes and were intent on discouraging the 10- and 15-yard passes, but their zone defenses left open the short areas.

Bill Walsh, with his West Coast offense, emphasized throwing very short passes, then counting on the receivers to gain their yardage by running after their catches.

The defenses had to match the offense's weapons. Four, and sometimes five or six, defensive backs replaced the normal three. The six- and seven-man defensive lines were reduced to three or four. From one or two linebackers, teams now use three or four as well. So teams moved from five pass defenders in the 1940s to seven or eight today. And while in the earlier days a pass rush would come from the six defensive linemen with an occasional "red dogging" linebacker, today any of the 11 defenders may be called on to blitz the passer. This requires the offensive teams to take time to learn to "pick up" the various blitzes. So you can see that as the offense changes to get an advantage, the defense changes to meet the challenge and to create more problems for the offense.

Blitz: A defensive play in which a linebacker or defensive back attacks past the line of scrimmage.

Dog or red dog: A linebacker attacking past the line of scrimmage at the snap of the ball.

With so many more variables on any one offensive or defensive play, coaches have had to build in "keys" for players so that they can adjust to situations after the ball is snapped. As an example on offense, a tight end may be required to watch a near linebacker on a pass play. If the linebacker blitzes, the end would yell "hot" and release to the zone that the backer can no longer cover. No matter what pass play has been called, the passer immediately throws to his "hot receiver."

Hot receiver: A receiver who becomes open because the defender who would have covered him has stunted into the offensive backfield.

Tight end: A receiver playing close to the offensive tackle.

Key: Watching an opponent to determine what he or his team will be doing.

Another offensive adjustment can be found in the post-read pass pattern. Against a four-deep alignment, the wide receiver starts downfield. If the defense is in a zone defense, the safety will either cover the flat short zone ("sky" cover) or the cornerback will cover it ("cloud" cover). If the receiver sees the safety coming laterally to cover the short flat zone, he breaks inside the cornerback, toward the goalposts. The quarterback has been making the same read, so he delivers the ball immediately. If the safety starts back to cover the deep outside zone, the receiver breaks to the corner. He will be wider than the safety. If it is a man-to-man defense, the receiver hooks at about 18 yards and comes back to the passer. Whatever the defense does is wrong!

Read: Getting an idea of what the opponents are doing by looking at one or more of them as the play develops. It can be done by defenders watching offensive linemen or backs or by passers and receivers watching pass coverage defenders.

Pre-snap read: A cue of defenders' intent evaluated by the quarterback or receivers based on the alignment of the pass defenders.

Guards: The offensive linemen on either side of the center.

On the defensive side of the ball, an inside linebacker might read the guard. If the guard blocks straight ahead, the backer comes forward. If the guard pulls laterally, the backer follows in that direction and attacks the ballcarrier. If the guard steps back in pass protection, the backer starts back into his zone and immediately checks the fullback. If the fullback steps outside it will be a pass. But if he stays in one spot or only moves a half step it will likely be a draw play, so the backer comes up to stop the run.

Some offensive and defensive ideas are recycled, often inadvertently. Others are novel, such as zone blocking, the option play, and passers and receivers reading the defense and adjusting the pass patterns after the ball is snapped.

In zone blocking, two adjacent offensive linemen block a defensive lineman, but they both watch the nearest linebacker to see which way he will run, then the nearest lineman to the linebacker's path comes off his block on the lineman and blocks the linebacker instead. In "option" plays the quarterback looks at a defensive lineman, usually a defensive end, then as he runs at the end he has the option of keeping the ball if the end doesn't try to tackle him, or pitching the ball to a trailing back. The defensive end can't cover both offensive players.

On pass plays both the receivers and the passer watch the movement of the pass defenders. If they see man-to-man coverage they know what fakes will most effectively free the receiver. If they see one of the more common zone defenses they must recognize where the seams are between the defenders in the zones. They then maneuver to move to those seams.

Option play: A play in which the quarterback runs at a wide defender, forcing the defender to either tackle him or stop the pitch to a trailing back. The quarterback can keep or pitch.

Zone blocking: Two adjacent offensive linemen double-team a down lineman, while both watch the backer. Whichever direction the backer moves, the nearest lineman releases and blocks him. The rule is "four hands on the lineman, four eyes on the backer."

Today's Game and Some Simplified Rules

The Field

The field is 300 by 160 feet with 30-foot end zones behind each goal line. There are "hash marks" marked in from the sideline where the ball is put in play after any down in which the ball becomes dead wider than the hash marks. This allows the offensive team some room to set its formation without being cramped by a sideline too near. In high school the hash marks are a third of the field in, 53⅓ feet. For college they are 60 feet in, and for the pros 70¾ feet.

Down: A play that begins after the ball is stopped. There are two types of downs, a scrimmage down and a free-kick down.

Hash marks: Short lines parallel with the sidelines that intersect each five-yard mark on the field. For high school the hash marks are a third of the field in, 53⅓ feet. For college they are 60 feet in, and for the pros 70¾ feet.

Downs

The ball can be advanced by running, passing, or kicking. After receiving a kick, the offensive team has four tries (downs) to gain 10 yards. If 10 yards are gained the team gets another first down to gain another 10 yards. If a team does not believe it can gain the 10 yards, it can kick (punt) the ball to the other team. Most teams will wait for the fourth down to kick, but they can kick on any down. Rain, a heavy wind, or being deep in one's territory are situations that could prompt an early punt.

Points

Scoring is done by running over the goal line with the ball or catching a thrown ball over the goal line. This is a touchdown and scores six points. After a touchdown the ball is put on the three-yard line. If the offensive team kicks the ball over the goal crossbar it is one extra point. If the team runs or passes the ball over the goal line the team gets two extra points. If a ballcarrier is tackled behind his own goal line it is considered a "safety," and the defensive team is awarded two points.

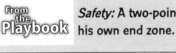

Safety: A two-point play that occurs when an offensive player is tackled behind his own end zone.

Positions

Eleven players are on the field for each team at one time. Substitutes are often brought into the game when situations change, such as for offense, defense, or different kicking situations.

Offense. On offense at least seven players must be within one foot of the line of scrimmage. The center is flanked by two guards, who are flanked by the tackles. The end players on the line are appropriately called ends. They and the four backs are eligible to catch forward passes. All players can catch balls thrown backward. The backs are called the quarterback, fullback, and two halfbacks. But these may take on other names, such as when ends or halfbacks are set out wide and are called wideouts or flankers. A halfback who is set deep may be called a tailback, or if set near a tight end he would be called a wingback. The backs are usually numbered from 1 to 49, the center in the 50s, the guards in the 60s, the tackles in the 70s, and the ends in the 80s.

Wideout: A split end or flanker on the offense, primarily used as a receiver.

Wingback: A back lined up about a yard wider and a yard deeper than the tight end.

The offensive linemen are the most important unit on the team and the most difficult to coach. They are normally the most intelligent players on the team. Intelligence is essential in recognizing the defensive alignment, immediately recognizing its strengths and weaknesses, determining which blocking scheme will work best—that is, which offensive linemen will block which defenders— and what techniques will be most effective. All of this has to be determined in four to eight seconds.

Offensive Players and Their Likely Numbers

The *Center*, the snapper, usually numbered in the 50s, is generally in the center of the line, but coaches may use an unbalanced line that would put him one or two places over, lining up in the guard or tackle position.

Guards generally flank the center, but in an unbalanced line they would both be on the same side of the center. They are usually numbered in the 60s.

Tackles are outside the guards. Some coaches will put both tackles, rather than both guards, on the same side of the center in an unbalanced line. They are usually numbered in the 70s.

Ends are the widest players on the offensive line. If an end is within a yard of the tackle he is called a tight end. If he is split wide he may be called a split end, wide receiver, flanker, or wideout. Typically the ends are numbered in the 80s.

Backs are categorized as quarterback; running backs (if they are set two to eight yards deep and inside the tackles); or wingbacks (if they are about a yard deep and a yard outside of the widest lineman, a tight end, or a tackle, if the end is split; or if they are split wide as wideouts, flankers, or wide receivers); and may be called slot backs or "Z" backs (if they are between the wide receiver and the widest lineman). Backs can have any numbers, but quarterbacks will usually have numbers below 10, and fullbacks will commonly use numbers in the 30s.

Slot: A back lined up in the area between a split end and the tackle.

The quarterback is the primary passer and team leader. Most teams play him just behind the center, where the center hands him the ball to start the play. Often teams will move him back about four yards into a "shotgun" formation. Most teams use him only as a passer in this formation, but many high school and college teams have him run or pass from this "spread" formation.

In the earlier days the backs were the quarterback, two halfbacks, and a fullback. The halfbacks lined up about four yards behind the tackles, and the fullback was about four yards behind the center. The fullback is now often moved up a yard or so and is primarily a blocker and a short-yardage ballcarrier. He is sometimes set a yard or two wider in what we call an "offset" position. Since one halfback is usually removed to a flanker position, it leaves only one halfback to run the ball. He is almost always set six to eight yards behind the center and is now called the tailback, rather than halfback. Sometimes the fullback and tailback are both set out as wide receivers. We call this an "empty" backfield.

Defense. The defensive team members can be aligned in any positions and can wear any numbers. However three to eight of them will be aligned within a foot or two of the line of scrimmage. They are there to stop the running plays and to rush or tackle the passer (a "sack"). One to five yards from the line of scrimmage one to four linebackers will set up. Their job is to help in stopping the runs, to protect against short passes, and sometimes to rush the passer. There are three to five or even six defensive backs. The cornerbacks are the widest and align near the widest receivers. They can align from a foot from the line of scrimmage to as deep as 10 yards. There will be one or two safeties. A free safety will align the deepest, usually from 8 to 15 yards. His primary job is to stop long passes. Another safety is called the strong safety. He too is there to stop longer passes, but he is also called on to support the run defense.

Sack: The tackling of the passer before he has a chance to pass.
Strong safety: The safety on the strong side (tight end) of the offense.

Defensive Players

The defensive line will have at least three players. Three or four are common today, five to seven were common in bygone days. The widest two are called defensive ends and commonly play over the offensive tackles. The inside players are called defensive tackles. In a three-man line the tackle will play on the nose of the center, and so is called a "nose tackle," although he may be "offset" to either side of the center. If there are two defensive tackles they will usually play over the guards, but they can be aligned on any offensive linemen. Their job is to stop the run and rush the passer.

The linebackers have the most difficult jobs. They must stop the runs, play pass defense in the short zones, and sometimes play man-to-man defense. While teams may play with from one to five backers, three or four are most common.

There are generally four defensive backs. The two widest defensive backs are the cornerbacks, and the two inside defensive backs are the safeties. One is the free safety and is often the deepest player in pass defense. The other safety is the strong safety. He lines up on the strong side of the formation and generally has some run responsibility.

Line of Scrimmage

Whenever a ballcarrier is stopped, the ball is placed wherever it was when the ballcarrier was tackled or ran out of bounds. The placement of the ball determines the line of scrimmage or the neutral zone. The line of scrimmage is a zone bounded by the two ends of the ball that extends to both sidelines and to the sky. If the next play is an incomplete pass, the ball is returned to the same line of scrimmage. Only the snapper, usually the center, can put his hands into this zone. Anyone else putting any part of his body into the zone before the ball is snapped is guilty of encroachment and is "offside."

Encroachment: Entering the neutral zone (the line of scrimmage bounded by the two ends of the ball) before the ball is snapped. It is a penalty in high school football. At the college and pro level it is a penalty only if contact is made with the other team.

Football has often been called a "contact" sport. But dancing can also be called a contact sport. Football might more properly be categorized as a "collision" sport. Offensive players collide with defenders when they block them, and defenders collide with offensive players when they tackle the ballcarrier. Blocking and tackling are the real essence of the game.

Formations

The offensive team must have at least seven players within a foot of the line of scrimmage. Before the ball is snapped all must remain motionless for at least one full second, however one back can be "in motion," laterally or backward, when the ball is snapped.

The Game

The kickoff starts each half of the game and begins play after every score.

The game lasts one hour, but the clock is stopped after every incomplete pass, whenever the ball goes out of bounds, when a first down is gained and the measuring chains must be moved, during penalty enforcement, and when a team calls a time-out. Because of the clock stoppages the actual game lasts longer than an hour. A high school game will generally run two to two and a half hours, and college and professional games will last three to four hours—depending on the number of passes thrown and the number of television commercials. If the game is being televised there will be additional time-outs for the commercials.

Penalties

Penalties are generally concerned with increasing the fairness of the game and reducing injuries. Penalties related to fairness include staying on one's own side of the line of scrimmage (no encroachment), not holding, preventing unfair shifting, not interfering with an eligible pass receiver, and so on. Penalties related to safety include no blocking in the back (clipping) and no blocking below the waist.

Clip: A block in which the defender is hit from behind. It is illegal.

The Equipment

As the game became more aggressive and injuries became a concern, players started adding protection—leather shoulder protection and leather head covering. These eventually became mandated. Now in high school and college a helmet, shoulder pads, and hip, knee, and thigh pads are required, along with a tooth protector and a face guard. These have reduced injuries, but as the shoulder pads became longer, the hip pads were embedded in a thick elastic jockey-short-type pant, and rib, back, elbow, and hand pads were added for more protection, it became more common for deaths and injuries to occur from dehydration and overheating than from trauma. There is just not enough open area to let the body's heat escape.

As you can see, the American variety of football is a complicated game. It involves a wide range of offensive and defensive possibilities, of team strategies and tactics, of individual techniques, of game preparation, and of a number of other factors that can change these possibilities. The weather, injuries, the arousal level of the players, the effectiveness of the coach's plans, and how well the team can execute those plans—all are factors in winning or losing the game.

CHAPTER 2

The Game in Our Society

Many people, maybe most, in every advanced society seem to have a great interest in some sport. In Europe, it is soccer (European football). In Norway, skiing often takes first place in the sports' derby. In Jamaica, they are justly proud of their sprinters, as are the Kenyans with their distance runners. In the States, football is king. High school students and communities often live or die with the success of their football teams. College students and alumni often judge their university in terms of its won-loss record on the gridiron. It shouldn't surprise anyone that the highest paid university employee in America is a football coach—Pete Carroll at the University of Southern California. His salary is 4.4 million dollars a year.

Football's Place in College Athletics

There are several levels of college athletic participation. The NCAA (National Collegiate Athletic Association) has three divisions. The NAIA (National Association of Intercollegiate Athletics) has two divisions. The NCAA Division 1 schools have athletic scholarships, and the NAIA schools offer some as well. Because of a court ruling (known as Title IX) that women are entitled to as many teams and scholarships as men, the schools had to come up with money for more scholarships, coaches, equipment, and travel. In many cases this led to a reduction of men's sports and scholarship money. In the largest Division 1A schools it fell on the football program to support the other sports. Some men's basketball programs support themselves, as do a few women's basketball programs. Seldom, if ever, do any of the other sports pay their own way.

With the pressure on the large-scale football programs to produce revenue, seasons were increased from 9 to 10, and eventually 11 games. The income from television became essential. So now we have college games on television all day Saturday, with additional games on Tuesday, Wednesday, and Thursday. The pros have been given Sundays, and it is hard for colleges to compete with "Monday Night Football." Fridays are supposed to be reserved for high school football, but often some colleges accept Friday night games, against the recommendation of the American Football Coaches Association.

The bowl games increased from one in 1902 to four for a number of years. Now there are enough games that every team with a winning record in Division 1A should get some bowl money. That income can range from a few hundred thousand dollars to several million. But a winning football team will bring in a great deal of money to the school from substantial donations of alumni and other interested people. It is no wonder that the top college coaches in Division 1A are paid up to $4 million a year. Even a few of the top assistant coaches earn a million a year. Of course coaches can be fired at any time—and unsuccessful ones may not even get to complete their contract. A few years ago two highly respected coaches at major universities were fired because they only won 8 of their 11 games—inexcusable for any coach to win fewer than all of his games! Then during the 2008 season a coach was fired in his ninth year because after bringing his team to a bowl game for eight consecutive years, his record in '08 was only 3–3.

Awards, Accolades, and Accomplishments

Americans, perhaps more than people from most countries, like awards and acclaim. Ten-year-old Pop Warner players all get large trophies for merely participating, while Olympic champions get a medal three inches in diameter. Every high school league and every college conference has its all-league or all-conference team. Then each city and state has its all-city and all-state team. Naturally there are All-American teams in every sport. Then there are the best-player awards. For college football it is the Heisman Trophy. For other leagues and conferences the award goes to the Most Valuable Player.

Obviously the heavy physical workload and the large time commitment force most football players to reduce their academic load during the season.

This often slows their progress toward the ideal four-year college graduation, so many athletes take five years. But there are exceptions, of course. Florida State safety and current Rhodes scholar Myron Rolle graduated in two and a half years as a premed major with an A-minus average. This exceptional student-athlete managed this feat while developing a health project for young Seminole Indian children, doing cancer research for a grant he received, and tutoring other students. Rolle is well on his way to fulfilling his dreams of having a career in the NFL, getting his M.D., and opening a clinic to help needy families in the Bahamas, where his family has roots.

Thirty-two students are awarded Rhodes scholarships annually. Of the other 16 men in the 2008 class, Christopher Joseph, a three-year offensive line starter for UCLA, and a UCLA rugby player were also chosen. Not a bad showing for the collision sport players.

Then there was Pat Tillman, who graduated summa cum laude in three and a half years while earning Pac Ten Defensive Player of the Year honors. He gave up a $4 million contract as a defensive back for the Arizona Cardinals to join the U.S. Army and fight in Afghanistan—a fight that cost him his life. His coach lamented, "He was a guy full of fiber—everything that he did went right to the core of what is good and sound in our country." Such accomplishments are the diamonds among the gold-plated trophies. And football was a significant contributor to the development of these heroes!

Playing the Game

General Douglas MacArthur said that football would never disappear from the U.S. Military Academy because it features both physical courage and the elements of war. Strategy and tactics play a major role in football. Coaches from the youth level on up generally put all their plays and other information into offensive, defensive, and kicking game playbooks. The coaches all have these playbooks, and they will guard these books with their lives. They may or may not give them to the players, since players cannot take them onto the field during the game. For any one game only a small part of the total number of formations and plays will be listed in the game plan and utilized.

Passing plays often have a greater chance for a long gain than running plays, but they are more risky. When you pass four things can happen, and three of them are bad—an incompletion, an interception, or a quarterback sack.

Throughout the game coaches will make their offensive and defensive tactical decisions based on what appears to be safe or what appears to be a good gamble according to what the scouting reports have indicated that the opponents will do in a given situation. There are safe runs and passes, and there are risky runs and passes. A defensive team can "blitz" linebackers or defensive backs in hope of sacking the quarterback or tackling the runner for a loss. But when a defender blitzes he abandons his pass responsibility.

The Professional Game

In 1902 the original National Football League was formed. Several baseball teams also played in the league during their off-season. The World Series of Football was played by five teams. It is strange that to this day most Americans don't seem to question the idea of playing "world" championships without letting teams from other countries around the world compete! Anyway, the league ended up folding in two years. This NFL had nothing to do with today's NFL.

A four-time Yale All-American, "Pudge" Heffelfinger, was paid $500 under the table to play for the Allegheny Athletic Association in an 1892 game against the Pittsburgh Athletic Club. Pudge earned his keep, scooping up a fumble and scoring the touchdown that won the game 4–0. So by receiving payment for his services, Pudge was the first professional football player.

Ohio became a hotbed of football, so the next professional league started there. The Ohio League had teams from a number of towns. It was this league that, in 1922, became today's National Football League. Canton, Ohio, is the site of the NFL's Hall of Fame. It was Canton that signed Jim Thorpe to a pro contract in 1915. Jim was perhaps America's greatest athlete at the time, an All-American in football and the winner of the Olympic decathlon.

Over the years other professional leagues have come and gone. After World War II the All America Conference was formed. The Cleveland Browns, the Baltimore Colts, and the San Francisco 49ers were among its teams. When the conference broke up they were taken into the NFL. Then in 1960 the American Football League emerged. This was the fourth league to take this name. A number of outstanding players joined the league. After the 1966 season, the leagues played a championship. The NFL won easily the first two years. Then, after the 1968 season, Joe Namath led the underdog New York Jets to a big win over the Baltimore Colts. In a little over a year the two leagues merged.

The NFL is now 32 teams strong. It is a well-run business, having made football the number one spectator sport in the United States. It holds the autumn captive. Stadiums are filled. Television games keep fans on their sofas from early morning until late at night, and "Monday Night Football" is *the* event of weekday television. The Super Bowl is the most watched program of the year. The NFL has created a demand for football that seemingly cannot be quenched.

Several steps have been implemented to keep teams more equal. The owners share in revenue, there is a salary cap for the teams, and the draft of players gives the lowest-ranking team the first choice of the college stars.

The present commissioner of the NFL, Roger Goodall, is making a strong effort to police the behavior of some of the pro players. It seems that paying them millions of dollars a year and giving them huge amounts of publicity goes to the heads of a few of the players. There are some people who still believe that athletes, pro and college, should be role models. The antisocial behavior of a few occasionally gives the whole league, and all of football, a poor image. Good sportsmanship is a worthwhile ideal—and antisocial behavior may well turn parents away from the stadium and the television.

Youth Football

High School Football

Every year more than a million boys, as well as a few girls, play high school football. Football is the most popular sport in high schools in the United States. More than 13,000 high schools participate in football, and in some places these teams play in stadiums that rival college-level facilities. For many towns, the whole year revolves around the success of the local high school teams.

At the high school or other junior levels, the game may be played with fewer people. Eight-man football has been a common game in small high schools.

More recently nine- and six-man games have developed. In the nine-man game you merely drop out the tackles. For the six-man game you have three linemen and three backs.

Youth Tackle Football

American football is a popular participation sport among youth. Flag and tackle football leagues are found in most communities. One of the earliest youth football organizations was founded in Philadelphia, in 1929, as the Junior Football Conference. It was soon renamed the Pop Warner Conference. Other leagues have been sponsored by police departments, religious groups, and recreation departments.

Today, the Pop Warner program enrolls more than 300,000 young boys and girls ages 5 to 16 in more than 5,000 football and cheerleading squads. The teams are financed and administered locally.

Touch Football

When boys or girls, from 6 to 60, want to play football in the streets or parks and don't want to tackle, they play "touch" football. The "tackle" is effected by touching with one or two hands, either below the waist or on any part of the body.

Flag Football

Flag football is played widely in physical education classes, intramural games, and youth leagues. Its players range from age six to adults. Coed leagues of flag football often start with six-year-olds. Now there is a movement, sponsored by the NFL, to have girls play interscholastic flag football in all-girl leagues as well as in coed games.

Spectators, Bands, and Cheerleaders

Naturally, when Rutgers played Princeton there were students who wanted to witness the mayhem. There is even more interest when one's classmates are playing, especially when they are playing for the honor and glory of dear old

Siwash! Look at the huge student body sections when UCLA plays USC, when Michigan plays Ohio State, when Yale plays Harvard—and there is nothing like the pride and excitement generated when Army plays Navy.

With all that enthusiasm, there must be someone to direct the exuberance to excite the players on the field. This task was originated by some young lads who called themselves cheerleaders. Some cheers were very specific, like "*Dee*-fense!" or "Touchdown!" or "First and ten—do it again!" But sometimes the yells had no special meaning. For example, the University of California at Davis was originally an agricultural school. The Aggies had a meaningless yell that captivated all who heard it. It went this way: "Oleo Margarine, Oleo Butterine, Alfalfa, Hay!" (That was in the days when Oleo was the major brand of margarine.)

Historically Speaking The "wave" has been used by the Seattle Seahawks since 1981. Television spread the stadium-wide phenomenon of successive section-by-section coordinated alternating standing and sitting. It was actually started a week before the Seahawks used it across town at the University of Washington by cheerleader Rob Weller, later the host of "Entertainment Tonight." The wave has spread from team to team and across the world—even finding its way to Olympic stadiums.

All-male cheerleading was infiltrated by females in the late 1940s. First girls became song leaders who danced to the "fight songs" played by the college bands. Soon the girls had pushed the boys off the cheerleaders' ramp. Then many of the cheers became so complicated that no one but the cheerleaders knew them. After a while, in the good old American way, cheerleading became its own sport with national and even international championships. Then to do the football players "one better," their sport became far more dangerous than the sport they were cheering for. In fact, cheerleading is now the most dangerous competitive sport in the schools and colleges. Cheerleaders may not be caught when thrown into the air, or one of their human pyramids may collapse.

Men have now rejoined the women as cheerleaders. In point of fact, however, they were never out of the picture. There have always been male cheerleaders, but with the emergence of the gymnastics-oriented performances of the girls and women, it was natural that men would join the acrobatics.

The college marching band has been around about as long as the football team. Commonly there are more band scholarships than football scholarships. The bands also often spend more hours practicing. When you see the high-stepping 200-member bands from Grambling or Southern, or watch a Big Ten band marching down the field in the shape of a Mississippi riverboat with the tuba players as the slowly rotating paddle wheel, you have witnessed a spectacle that may rival the game for excitement!

The American brand of football and its accoutrements have spread across much of the world with its forward pass and its cartwheeling cheerleaders. So hooray for the games of football! Now let's get on with looking at our American game, particularly 11-man tackle, in more detail. It is always best to understand the "whys and hows." So here we go with a deeper look at football—for the utterly confused.

PART II

The Whys and Hows of the Xs and Os

CHAPTER 3
A Philosophy of Coaching and Playing

We want to give you a "coach's eye" view of the game. As good as the players are at what they do, few understand the big picture. As a spectator, a parent of a player, a flag football player, or a youth coach, you want to see the whole picture. And the whole picture begins with the philosophy of the coach.

The great conductor Franz Schalk once said, "Every theatre is an insane asylum, but an opera theatre is the ward for the incurables." The same might very well be said about football coaches and the players at the higher levels—for a multitude of reasons, *football is fun*!

Every type of game excites its participants. Whether it is Monopoly, hide-and-seek, or football, people play for the enjoyment. Those of us who have made lifelong commitments to the game of football have deep attachments to this very special game. And the people who have the deepest attachment to football are probably the sport's coaches.

There is no question that successful coaches are winners—but that winning doesn't always show on the scoreboard. Dr. Gloria Balague, one of the world's top sport psychologists, lists these essentials of coaching:

- The coaching process must emphasize the development of character.

- The coach must be competent in the necessary knowledge for the appropriate level for the sport.

- The coach must be committed to helping the players learn.

- The coach must really care for the players.

- The coach must build confidence in the players.

- The coach must be an effective communicator, knowing when to say nothing, when to praise, and how to criticize.

- The coach must be consistent in attitude and discipline.

For youth coaches, the younger the players, the more parents should be involved. Parents should know the direction the coach wants to take in developing their children. Sometimes the importance of the scoreboard has to be reduced in the coach's or a parent's mind. The "win at all costs" attitude at the pro level, and to a large degree at the college level, often works its way down to the high school and youth league levels. Does the coach have a "win at all costs" mentality, or is the education of the players his or her primary objective?

The values that can be taught through football include not only setting goals for the season and working hard to achieve them, but also avoiding cheating, practicing good sportsmanship, and achieving better academic progress. But you well know that the coach must live the values he or she is trying to teach. We all learn better by watching than by hearing.

Keep paramount in your mind that it is all about the players—as long as they are not getting paid to play. When they are professionals we expect success. But even here the coach is responsible for helping them to be successful. The motivation to be successful and to win actually increases as a player moves up the talent scale. The coach at the pro level is at least as concerned with motivation and fundamentals as is the high school or youth coach.

If you are coaching, what is it that you want to teach: blocking and tackling, life values, a passing attack, developing a work ethic, goal setting and the motivation of working toward goals in football and/or in life, playing pass defense, making every player feel important? Coaches don't have time to teach everything well, so they must be clear on which lessons are most important for them to impart. Coaches aim for success. But how do we measure our success—in championships or in the positive development of players toward success in life? While some may emphasize one or the other, these goals are not mutually exclusive. But whatever the goals, one must plan for both the content and the methods of teaching. It doesn't just happen.

Experience tells us that when the game is set into the wider picture of life, of how to live more effectively, of setting high goals and working toward them, of the players seeing themselves as part of a team, rather than the all-important individual, the game becomes bigger than life and the chances for success on the field are substantially increased.

When pro, college, high school, or youth coaches hold players out of a game because they have broken rules or exhibited selfish attitudes, the player and the teammates learn life lessons and the team emerges as a stronger entity. Coaches often have to play the part of the fathers or mothers who may not have instilled effective values into their sons or daughters. You have heard the saying that there is no *I* in *team*. When individual selfishness pollutes team goals, team cohesion is weakened. And it is team cohesion, not the Xs and Os, that wins games and develops character.

The Soul of the Game

Your philosophy is why you coach or play the game. What result should you be looking for? Every player and every coach learns something every year from the game. Sometimes what's learned is negative. Hopefully the great majority of experiences will be positive. It is the coach's job to ensure that the experiences of his or her players are primarily of a positive variety.

Certainly we don't want our children to be losers, but we don't want them to win and become conceited either. We shouldn't encourage them to play high school football just so they will get a college scholarship or become a pro player. A few years ago, in his keynote address to the American Football Coaches Association, former Chicago Bear defensive standout and Pro Hall of Famer Mike Singletary said, "If anyone would ask me what coaching really means, it's not really about winning. It's not really about Xs and Os. All those things go into it, but it's about influence." He then went on to say, "The coach would push them, would test them, would take them to the next level. But most importantly, love them." At the time Mike wasn't involved in coaching, but now he is the head coach of the San Francisco 49ers.

He went on to say that a vision is needed for everything that is important to accomplish. "I had the vision of what I wanted to do when I was growing up. I wrote it down and put it on my wall. But people saw it and laughed, so I put it in my closet. I am so thankful that at that time in my life I made the decision to make a commitment. If you don't commit, it won't happen." Whether it's family or football, work or religion, you have got to be committed.

Coaches have a deep responsibility to their players. It is their job to know the young people they're teaching, the game itself, and how the game of football can bring players to their highest potential as happy and contributing citizens, husbands, and fathers.

The Theory of the Game

A coach's theory is the overall approach he takes to winning. As a coach, on offense, do you try to get a first down on every series (as most teams do), or do you play a more conservative "field position" game while attempting to eliminate mistakes and capitalize on those of the opponents? On defense, do you attack and gamble on creating losses, or merely attempt to limit the opponent's gains for three downs, then force a fourth-down punt? How important is the kicking game—is it a necessary evil while waiting to play offense, or is it a key part of your approach to winning the game? These are very real considerations—each approach has its advantages.

In this book we just want to give you a picture of a number of options that coaches can choose. Understanding these should give you a greater appreciation of the game. If you were the coach, how would you use your practice time? There is never enough time to practice everything, and teams tend to do well with what they practice well. Since time is the coach's currency, he must decide how to spend it effectively.

For instance, the punt is the most important play in football. This fact raises a lot of questions about how the coach should spend time during practice. How much time should be spent long snapping, punting, and blocking the various defenses that might rush the punt? Turnovers, pass interceptions, and fumbles are big gainers for the opposition. How much time should you spend reducing turnovers? How much time should you spend increasing the other team's turnovers by working on stealing the ball or intercepting passes? How much time should you spend reducing your own team's penalties?

Pro coaches have all year to work on some aspects of the game. Colleges and high schools are limited in the number of weeks and the number of hours in a week that they can practice, so the coach must decide how to make the best use of this time.

Strategy and Tactics

Strategy is one of the most interesting parts of the game. After scouting the opposing team, the coach will attempt to find how he can match his team's strengths against the weaknesses of his opponent—in personnel, formations, and situations.

Tactics, adjusting to unanticipated changes during a game, are often the key to winning—especially in close games. Here is where knowledge and experience really count in coaching. How can a coach cope with the opponent's unexpected changes in attack and defense? If an injury occurs to either team, how will that change his plans? These are things every coach must anticipate before every game.

So, coaching is a mix of many things that each coach blends in his own way. No two coaches or programs are identical. What will a particular coach's stamp bring to the athletes? Bobby Bowden said that he sees the essentials of coaching as honesty, loyalty, and compassion. The essentials for players are to be unselfish, to be a team player, and to love their teammates. The team, not the individual, must be primary in football.

A Football Game Is More than a Jousting Match

When coaches talk about winning, you will hear a number of factors emphasized. Each is true. You have probably heard that "Football is a game of inches" or that "Coaching is a race against time." One of the coach's concerns is gaining the most inches and yards in the shortest amount of time. But just as accurate is the reality that a football game is much more than 60 or 70 plays run successively to test a team's execution—rather it is a kaleidoscope of ever-changing situations. A team's ability to simultaneously execute assignments and fundamentals while recognizing and managing game situations is what determines its performance.

When we watch a football game we see blocking and tackling on every play. This is the hard physical "colliding" part of the game. The "jousting" part of the game, the necessity to beat a player physically, is the essence of the game, but it is not *the game*. Just like catching a ball is not baseball but is essential to the game. And shooting a basket is not basketball but is essential to the game. Blocking or beating a block, tackling or evading a tackle, catching a pass or making an interception are all parts of the physical aspect of the game—the joust. But the game is much more complicated than just the joust!

Coaches want to find the winning edge. They need to practice the things that will win when their defense is not overpowering or their offense is stumbling or fumbling. The game has changed since the days of the flying wedge. It goes well beyond the jousting contests of blocking and tackling.

Fundamentals Are *Fundamental*!

Walking is fundamental to running—but it isn't running. Blocking and tackling are fundamental to playing the game of football—but they are not *the game*. As a player, if you can't block and tackle, you can't play the game of tackle football. Certainly the fundamentals are important at every level of football. All-Pro linebacker Matt Millan answered, when asked what he did when things were not going well in a game, "First I check my stance, then I check my reads, then I evaluate my reactions to the opponent's plays." Fundamentals are critical at any level of play—and in everything worthwhile that we do. The three *R*s (readin', writin', and 'rithmatic) are fundamental to learning, and learning is fundamental to becoming an effective member of society. Fundamentals are essential to everything we do—if we want to do it effectively.

Executing the Fundamentals

Effective play execution is another essential of winning in football—as it is in other sports. Since football is probably the most complicated and interesting of all games, it takes more than merely perfecting the fundamentals. Certainly blocking, tackling, throwing, catching, and kicking are absolutely essential to playing the game. But just as having a strong forehand and backhand is essential to a tennis player, it is how and when you use them that is essential to the game.

In track and field, because athletes just run or jump or throw, fundamentals and conditioning are nearly all there is to the competition. But when you are playing a game you will find more situations that must be successfully encountered. In an individual game like tennis, winning the situation often wins the match. As we move to team games, the individual situations take on an ever-increasing importance—and become absolutely critical to winning.

In football, coaches must understand and teach their players how to play the *game*. This game, after all, is the most complex game ever invented. It has more circumstances, more variables, and more players than other games, and every play is a chess match that can result in a win or a loss—depending on who plays correctly and who makes a mistake. The coach must be an engineer who builds a team that performs efficiently in all of the intricacies of the game. It is the coach's job to develop in his team that *collective mentality* that will help to win the various situations that can come up in every game.

Practicing the situations is of major import for every coach. At the pro level there is more time to practice these small things that win big—the "impact area" of the game. Youth, high school, and college teams have less time to practice them, but they must be practiced. It may be practicing offense or defense for third and long situations. It may be scoring or preventing a score from the three-yard line. It may be attempting to get into field goal range from 70 yards out with 45 seconds remaining in the game. The head coach, the assistants, and the team members must all be on the same page, have the same collective mentality, if they are to play the game as a unified team.

Field goal: A ball placekicked or drop-kicked over the goalposts. It scores three points.

Planning for and Winning the Impact Areas of the Game

Coaches must have a clear mental picture of how they want their team to behave. When a coach has that picture, he can build on the vision and develop that collective mentality. But if he doesn't have that complete vision, or if he has it but doesn't impart it to the players, then it is ridiculous to pound the table after the game and yell, "If we had only done this" or "If only that guy hadn't run out of bounds."

As in all walks of life, we have to practice our vision. As a coach, you shouldn't blame your players if they haven't practiced a situation. Telling them what to do during a time-out is not enough. If you could tell them and they could do it perfectly, there would be no need to practice. You could just give them a book of your instructions and have them come back on game day.

Coaches who berate their teams for not doing things that they haven't practiced are no better than the second-guessers, the armchair quarterbacks who know how to handle every situation—after it has already happened. The effective coach must anticipate what might happen, then practice effectively to prepare for those possibilities. It is the coach's job to have a "grand plan" to allow enough time for the players to learn how to handle the "what-ifs" of the game.

Many games are won in the last two minutes. Television announcers talk about the "two-minute drill." But it is really what the coaches call the two-minute situation. The two-minute situation has many possibilities. As a coach, what if you run the draw play on first down and make 50 yards? You didn't expect it, but here you are on the opponent's 12-yard line. At the pro level you must practice this exact situation. If you break a big play in the two-minute situation, you want your team's collective mentality to be ready to react. A good team isn't surprised by success.

Most teams are not going to score on every possession. The opportunities for a long drive are often frustrated by an offensive penalty, a turnover, a big defensive play such as a blitz, or not converting on a third down. Just as the game of golf is theoretically quite simple—just hit the ball into the hole—in actuality you never have the same shot twice. One time it is an uphill lie 190 yards from the pin on the fourth hole of Spyglass, the next time it is a 191-yard uphill lie on the seventh fairway at St. Andrews. These are two very different shots. Football is the same. A third and four on your own 40 when ahead against the Dolphins is not the same as a third and four on your own 40 when ahead against the Bears.

Winning is more than just fundamentals and execution. Even a highly motivated, highly skilled team can get beaten consistently if the players don't know how to deal with the things that happen during the game.

Winning Isn't Everything

The goals of winning through hard work and overcoming adversity are essentials in a democratic capitalistic society. Football, properly taught, is a perfect vehicle to develop the feelings of cooperation and competition, of aggression and compassion, and of the joys of winning and the sorrows of losing. Football teaches a player how to be a successful person in our society better than any other subject in the school curriculum.

Football is the great American game—not only because of its popularity in the stadium and on television but also because of what it does for the youth of the country. Can football help to keep America tough with its eyes on the future? We think that it can—and does.

CHAPTER 4
Theories of Winning

An intelligent coach does not just sit down and wildly draw Xs and Os; there must be a method in the madness. First he must determine the overall theory of how he wants to win, or how he wants to avoid losing.

Intelligent football coaches (just as heads of state, generals, and business administrators do) must have an overall theory of how they expect to win. Since practice time is limited, coaches must determine their general approach to the game so that the alignments, plays, and skills required can be designed and practiced.

Some emphasize their defensive talents, some count on their knowledge of the kicking game, but most count on their offensive ideas to produce their victories. Some believe that the best defense is a good offense. Others believe that the best offense is a good defense. Advocates of both positions have won national and professional championships.

Field Position Theory

The field position theory of winning is probably as old as the game. Whether it was Knute Rockne, Red Sanders, or Darrell Royal—most of the legendary coaches of college football have been field position advocates.

Those who emphasize position football generally want to keep their opponents bottled up in their own territory. It is their belief that it is extremely difficult to march a team 70 or 80 yards for a touchdown. The odds are that somewhere during that march there will be a penalty, a fumble, an incomplete pass, or an interception that will stop the drive. Field position advocates place their hopes in the old adage that "to err is human" and hope that their opponents are particularly "human" on game day.

By emphasizing defense and kicking they hope to be able to slow down their opponents and to force the miscue that will result in a stalled drive or a turnover. These coaches will generally put their best players on the defensive team. They will also spend a great deal of time perfecting the kicking game, especially punting.

 The 2003 Ohio State team is a perfect case study of "field position" football. Jim Tressel's team played strong and kept its opponents pinned back, winning three games without scoring an offensive touchdown.

Likelihood of Scoring a Touchdown

Naturally, the closer to the goal the possession starts, the greater the odds of scoring. Most teams are not going to score on every possession. This means that a punt or field goal must be attempted.

Jimmy Johnson, Cowboy Super Bowl coach, charted the following statistics for the pros:

- From their own goal line to the −25, the average team will score 7 to 12 percent of the time.

- From the −25 to the 50, the average team scores 25 to 30 percent of the time.

- From the 50 to the +25, the average teams scores 45 to 60 percent of the time.

- From the +25 to the goal line, the average team scores 80 percent of the time.

Frank Beamer of Virginia Tech finds the college probabilities lower. From inside your own 20 he sees a 3 percent chance of scoring a touchdown. From the −20 to −40 there's about a 12 percent chance, at the 50 about 20 percent, at the +40 it rises to 33 percent, at the +20 it is 50 percent, and if you get the ball at the opponent's 10-yard line your chances of scoring are about 50 percent.

George O'Leary, head coach at the University of Central Florida, has developed a scoring percentage chart based on analyzing 10,000 plays. His scoring percentages (touchdown or field goal) are very similar to Johnson's and Beamer's. O'Leary's percentages were only for the "minus" side of the 50:

Likelihood of Scoring						
Johnson	0 to −25	−25 to 50	50 to +25	+25 to goal		
(pros)	7–12%	25–30%	45–60%	80%		
Beamer	Goal to −20	−20 to −40	50	+ 40	+20	+10 to goal
(college)	3%	12%	20%	33%	50%	50%
O'Leary	−10	−40	at 50-yard line			
(college)	2.5%	11%	25%			

Increasing and Decreasing the Likelihood of a Touchdown

Many coaches believe that it isn't so often that one team "wins" the game as that the other team "loses" it. This is particularly true in close games. So the field position advocates try to "not lose" the game. With the ball inside their own 10-yard line, they may punt it on first down. Inside their 20, they may punt on second down, and inside their 35 on third down. Of course, since they spend so much time on the kicking game they may well surprise their opponents by a fake punt on first, second, or third down. If the opponents send back one or two safetymen to field the punt, they are weakened against the run and the pass—so an occasional fake might get good yardage.

The field position coaches will generally divide the field into specific areas. As has been noted, inside their 35-yard line is going to be an early kicking down, that is, a punt on first, second, or third down. From the 35 to the 50 is an area in which "safe" plays are called. Once past midfield, they will probably open up and may throw some passes. Then inside their opponent's 35-yard line they will generally assume that they are in "four down territory," where they only have to make two and a half yards per play to score. So they may revert to a more conservative running game.

Knute Rockne divided the field into five 20-yard areas. From his own goal to the 20 he would kick on first down. From his 20 to his 40 he wouldn't pass and would punt on second or third down. Between the 40s he might pass and would punt only on fourth down. From the offensive 40 to the 20 he would use some trick plays and would use a field goal if his offense was stopped. From the 20 to the goal he would use the plays most likely to score.

Darrell Royal, the former Texas coach, thought in terms of three zones. From his goal to the 35 he wanted to get the ball across the 50 in any way possible—safe runs, passes, and if necessary, the punt. Between the 35s he called "the alumni zone," where it was the duty of the coach to entertain the fans with passes and trick plays. From the offensive 35 on in it was four down territory, and the team had to score.

Most field position coaches used colors to denote the area of the field in which they had the ball. It might be red for danger near the goal line they were protecting. Or it might be yellow for caution. Orange might be used in the middle of the field, then green for "Go" or red for blood near the team's goal line. It is this last "red zone" concept as you near your goal line that has now become the standard lingo. So even teams that do not label other areas of the field now nearly universally use the term "red zone" as they near their goal line.

Red zone: The area from the 20- or 25-yard line to the goal line. The most critical area for both the offense and the defense.

One advantage of field position football comes when playing on a soggy field. A team could punt on an early down, let the opponent fumble or have a punt blocked, then power the ball in for the touchdown. Of course if the team can't play good defense, this strategy won't work. But it can be a very effective strategy. The pros, with their usually high-scoring offenses, fields under tarps or domes, and fresh balls on every play, wouldn't use this approach. In fact, the pro approach is usually that it is to the offense's advantage to play on a wet field because the pass defenders have a better chance to be defeated.

Since a game of college football generally involves more than 130 plays with 22 players on each play, there are ample opportunities for errors. The old coaching adage that "football is a game of inches" indicates the small margin of error that can be the difference between winning and losing—and the field position coaches don't want to lose.

Ball Control Theory

The ball control coaches are more interested in offense—a safe offense. They hope to make three and a half yards on each of three running downs or five yards on two of their three passes so that they can get the first down. Naturally they want to avoid any mistakes such as penalties or turnovers.

When drawn on paper, every offensive play can easily gain four yards. On the blackboard, every lineman makes his block and the ballcarrier never fumbles. The problem for football is that offensive players seldom perform as well as the Os on the chalkboard. On the chalkboard the Os always beat the Xs—at least when the offensive coordinator has the chalk.

Winning with the Run or Pass

In analyzing the possibilities of these theories of winning, it should be noted that the rule changes regarding the use of the hands in blocking give the offense more advantage than it used to have over the defense. It also gives the pass protectors much more ability to protect the passer than they had when their hands had to remain close to the chest. Both the running game and the passing game are enhanced by the current use of the hands in blocking.

A major fascination with the pass is that it is fun to design. Coaches are notorious for drawing plays on everything from tablecloths to the palms of their hands. On the drawing board or napkin, every coach can theorize his way to the Super Bowl. Also, the players like to practice passing. It is a rare event when boys will go down to the park to block each other, but they will leave at the drop of a hat to "throw the ball around."

Then there is the weather factor. If your team plays in Nome, Alaska, or in Seattle you must be concerned with the cold or the rain. Both can affect your passing attack more than your running attack. If you are guaranteed to play every game on clear and windless 70-degree days, your chances of success for your passing attack are greatly increased.

We see so many teams passing that many people believe that passing is the best way to win. While most coaches express their hope for a "balanced" attack gaining nearly equal amounts of yardage from the run and the pass, in reality the running game has a lot going for it. In the college game the 10 top running teams in the country generally average 80 percent wins, but the 10 top passing teams generally average only 50 percent wins. At the pro level it has been found that teams that run 40 times in a game will win 90 percent of the time. Another pro statistic is that when the passer has a 300-yard game, his team wins 50 percent of the time. When a running back has a 100-yard day, the team will win 80 percent of the time. How many times does a team lose when one of its backs runs for more than 100 yards? Not often!

On the other hand, the short passing game has increased scoring to an average of more than 45 total points per game. With short passes becoming more like runs in terms of yards gained and the reduced interceptions, the pros and colleges are increasingly opting for the run and short pass approach.

The coach's decision on how his team can best win is essential in determining his theories of offense, defense, and kicking. It will also play an essential part in the development of his week-to-week strategy for upcoming opponents and in the tactical decisions he will make during each game. When a coach decides to punt on fourth and one on his opponent's 45, that decision was probably made months, or even years before, as part of his overall theory of winning. The "boos" from the stands will not persuade him to do otherwise.

Winning in Overtime

Originally football games could end in ties. This was fine when underdogs played the favorite to a tie—and a "moral" victory. But as playoffs toward championships increased, some way had to be found to determine which team would advance to the next round. Originally the team with the most first downs was chosen, but perhaps the other team had more total yardage. So overtime play was initiated. In 1941, with the Chicago Bears playing the Green Bay Packers for the NFL championship, the coaches agreed that if a tie occurred they would play an overtime tiebreaker. It wasn't necessary because the Bears won, but the next January at the meeting of the rules committee, an overtime rule was put in place for the pros.

The coin flip to start the overtime period is often the most important "play" of the period. For the pros it determines which team will receive the kickoff in the 15-minute sudden death period. Depending on the year surveyed, the winner of the coin toss wins 52 to 62 percent of the time. For colleges, the coin toss determines which team will start a series from the 25-yard line. For high schools it determines which team will start a series of downs from the 10-yard line. If the winner of the flip at the high school or college level chooses to go second, it knows how many points it needs to score to win or tie and send the game into an additional overtime period, as both teams have an equal number of chances to score. At the pro level the coin-toss winner may move right down the field for a touchdown or field goal—and that ends the sudden death overtime.

In a 2001 game between Arkansas and Mississippi, the score was tied 17–17 at the end of regulation time. Seven playoff periods later, Arkansas won 58–56, as Eli Manning, now with the New York Giants, threw five touchdown passes in the overtime periods.

Winning in overtime outside of the pro game does not require managing the clock as the last few minutes of a half may require. Depending on the circumstances, a team can use the run or pass to score, and if it hasn't scored by the fourth down a player can kick a field goal.

CHAPTER 5

Theories of Offensive Formations

Obviously a coach chooses a formation that will allow him to attack the opponents most effectively according to his theory of offense. Today's pro teams nearly always use a formation that will allow at least three immediate pass receivers into the defensive secondary, the area that begins two to four yards past the line of scrimmage.

From the Playbook

***Secondary:* The safetymen and cornerbacks.**

Before starting an offensive play, the coach or signal caller may choose a formation because it is especially advantageous for that play (such as a split back pro formation for a pass), or he may choose one just to see how the defense adjusts so that any weakness can be exploited on an ensuing play. For example, on an off-tackle power play there is an obvious advantage to having a tight wingback next to the end in order to double-team the defender (the reference to "power" in the name of the play comes specifically from this potentially powerful double-team block). If this is done, the defense must decide whether to adjust by bunching up to stop the obvious power of the formation but perhaps open itself to a pass from that formation as a result (if players are shifted to answer the double-team, a separate receiver might be left uncovered).

Tight formations have the advantages of running power, good faking, and quick counters, but they lack the quick wide pass threat. Teams with good passers and receivers are more likely to want at least three immediate receivers threatening the defense. They will also want to spread the defense from sideline to sideline so that the defense has more area to defend.

With the defense spread wide there are more possible openings between the defenders for the receivers to exploit.

A major reason for using varying sets and motions in a formation is to be able to get a mismatch. Offensive football is about gaining mismatches. For example, when in a passing situation, a mismatch may mean getting a faster receiver on a slower defender, a taller receiver on a shorter defender, a fresh receiver on a tired or injured defender, or getting more men to one side of the ball.

Spacing

The spacing of the linemen is another factor for a coach to consider. If the linemen are close to each other they can pass protect, double-team, zone block, and cross block more effectively. Also it is more difficult for the defenders to penetrate the offensive line of scrimmage. The backs can also get around the end faster on sweep plays because there's less of a line for them to get around. On the other hand, the defenders are all closer to the point of attack.

Sweep: A wide offensive power running play.

If the offensive linemen are split wider, they spread the defense better and create either holes or blocking angles. If the defensive lineman moves out with the offensive man, a hole is created. If the defender splits only partway, perhaps playing on the inside shoulder of the offensive man, a blocking angle is created.

It is obvious that if all three backs are set in the normal T formation there will be a great threat to the defense in quickness and countering. Each back removed from the three-back formation reduces the running attack while adding to the passing threat. When a coach decides to remove a fullback, he gives up the buck, the fullback trap, the fullback counter, and the fullback slant. When he removes a halfback, he gives up the dive threat and the quick pitch to that side and the halfback traps and counters to the other side. The defense knows this and can afford to reduce its defense in the areas where it is not threatened.

Dive: A quick straight-ahead play with the halfback carrying the ball.

Trap: Blocking of a defensive lineman by an offensive player who did not line up close to him originally. In a trap block the blocker will have his head on the defensive (downfield) side of the opponent, and the play is designed to go inside the block.

When a coach is running an I pro attack he may put his tailback from four and a half to as far as seven or eight yards back. If he wants the back to hit a certain hole, he will have him closer. But if he wants the back to pick his hole depending on how the defense adjusts to the play, the back will be deeper because holes may open at any point in the offensive line depending on who has blocked efficiently and how the defense has moved once the play has begun.

Pick: A pass pattern in which one of the potential receivers hits or screens off a defender, allowing his teammate to be free; also slang for an interception.

Shifting and Motion

As defenses became more specialized with a strong safety, strong corner-back, strong and weak linebackers, and perhaps strong and weak defensive linemen—all with special responsibilities—it was inevitable that someone would shift to upset such defenses. Since the defenders will declare the offense "strong" to the side of the tight end, many teams would start the tight end on one side, let the defense set, then move the tight end to the other end of the line. This movement of one offensive man could force the defense to move at least two defenders—and probably six or more men. This shift might force the movement of the strong and free safeties and the strong and weak inside and outside backers. In adjusting, the defense might align wrong or be too slow in making its adjustment and be therefore weakened and vulnerable to a special offensive play.

Historically Speaking Knute Rockne is given credit for perfecting the backfield shift. Bob Zuppke, at Illinois, used a line shift to help spring Red Grange to his legendary running exploits. The guards were set behind the line, and gaps were left on each side of the center. Then the guards shifted into the right or left gap to give an unbalanced line for the "Galloping Ghost" to run behind.

Perhaps no modern team has exploited the shift as much as the Dallas Cowboys did under Tom Landry. They would line up in one formation, then everybody would move. The linemen adjusted their splits, and the backs would move to another position. They knew where they were going, but the defense didn't.

From the Playbook *Unbalanced line:* An offensive alignment in which four or more linemen are set on one side of the line of scrimmage.

American football teams are allowed to have a back in motion going parallel to the line of scrimmage or moving backward. Motion can be used to change a formation by changing the strength of the formation (changing from a flanker to a slot or a slot to a flanker formation). When defenses don't adjust to the motion, they make themselves vulnerable to the offense changing the formation strength, then attacking toward that strength. It is amazing how often teams will disregard the change in formation strength.

Flanker: A back split wider than a wingback.

Another major use of motion is to determine whether the defense is playing a man-to-man or a zone defense on that play. This makes it easier for the quarterback and the receivers to determine which patterns will work best. If a zone shows (the motion back is not followed by a defender), perhaps a deep curl would be run. If man-to-man shows (a defender follows the motion man), perhaps a crossing pattern or a comeback would work best.

When you are watching a game, check the defensive adjustments to motion and you will be able to determine for yourself whether the team is playing zone or man-to-man defense.

Zone defense: A pass coverage in which the linebackers and defensive backs protect areas and play the ball rather than watch specific men.

Curl: A pass pattern in which the receiver runs 12 to 20 yards downfield and then comes back toward the passer in an open area of the defensive coverage.

Modern-day teams are usually multiple-formation teams that use a good deal of motion. A good part of the "chess match" element of the game is involved in setting one's formations, then evaluating the opponent's adjustments to them.

Finding and exploiting the weaknesses in a defensive team's adjustments to formations can often be the key to winning the offensive battle.

Coaches must be aware of the importance of choosing formations. Some coaches use only a few plays but many formations. By noting how the defense adjusts, the coach can get a good idea of where the defensive weaknesses will be with each offensive set. He can then set his formation and call a play that will attack the vulnerable area of the defense. Other coaches will use few formations, believing that they would rather know where the defense will be, then plan their attack.

CHAPTER 6

The Running Attack

A running play is based on power, quickness, or finesse. All coaches will use at least two of these theories, but in most offenses only one will be emphasized. The power game is predicated on the idea of having more men than your opponents at the point of attack. Most power teams will use double-team blocks by the linemen and/or blocking backs to accomplish this. Advocates of the quickness game will attempt to get the ballcarrier to the line of scrimmage before the defense has a chance to react and pursue. The halfback dive play, the fullback buck, and the quarterback sneak are examples of quickness plays. The finesse game utilizes deception or "reads" to fool the defense. Traps, counters, and reverses, as well as the various option series, fall into this category.

Power

The most powerful plays come from single wing attacks, with multiple double-team blocks and pulling linemen. The off-tackle power game from the T formation was probably best emphasized by Vince Lombardi's attack at Green Bay. The Green Bay "sweep" could be cut "off tackle" or continued as a wide sweep—depending on whether the outside linebacker was blocked out or in.

While at USC in the 1960s, John McKay combined the I formation with the pro-style wide receivers. This gained him a passing advantage while retaining much of the single wing power. The disadvantages of the I formation are that backs can't get outside quickly and it doesn't have the capability of crossing the backs in faking actions—so it is easier for the linebackers to key. The pros often still utilize John McKay's ideas today.

I formation: A formation in which the quarterback, fullback, and tailback are in a line.

Quickness

The quickness game is indigenous to the T formation. Because the center hands the ball to the quarterback, he can hand off to any of his other backs—without them having to wait for the ball to get to them, as in the single wing. With a quickness attack, most of the blocks will be one on one. And those blocks don't have to be sustained long because the back will be at the hole in about half a second. If the play is designed to hit between the guards, the fullback will probably carry it. If is to go just inside or outside of the tackle, the halfback will usually carry it. Getting wide quickly is done by pitching the ball quickly to a halfback who was aligned behind the tackle.

Finesse

Possibly the most finesse-oriented offense was the old Michigan unbalanced line buck-lateral series. The ball was snapped to the fullback, who dove into the line. The blocking back might lead him or turn and have the ball faked to him or given to him. If it was given to him, he might run into a different hole, drop back to pass, hand to the wingback on a reverse, or pitch to the tailback—

who might run wide or pass. The reverse or some sort of countering play is essential to this attack.

Another part of the finesse game involves what has come to be known as "option" football. In this type of attack the quarterback must determine whether to give or keep the ball depending on the action of a defensive player. On wide plays from the split T attack, the quarterback will fake to the diving halfback, then when he comes to the defensive end he has to decide whether to keep the ball himself and cut upfield or pitch to the trailing halfback. The man who is being optioned (in this case, the defensive end) is not blocked.

The ultimate in "option" football is the triple option. In a triple option both the defensive end and the tackle are left unblocked. A back dives into the line, and the quarterback determines whether the first unblocked lineman will tackle that back. If not, he hands the ball to the back. If the defender attacks the charging back, the quarterback keeps the ball and moves to the next unblocked defender. If the defender takes him, he pitches to the trailing back. If the defender does not take him, the quarterback keeps the ball. This all happens in a second to a second and a half. Because there are two unblocked linemen, there are extra offensive linemen who can double-team the opposing defenders, especially the linebackers. This gives this type of finesse attack some of the elements of a power attack.

Historically Speaking

Utah's and Florida's highly effective offenses feature the quarterback running from the shotgun, then having the option to pitch to a trailing back or forward to another eligible receiver who is being accompanied by a pulling lineman. Most teams that use a spread or shotgun offense will use an option play with the quarterback heading toward the defensive end, then having the option of pitching to the other back.

The most common finesse play seen today starts with the ballcarrier six to eight yards deep, then running behind zone blocking and picking his hole, which is often on the back side of the formation. This requires great vision by the ballcarrier. This deep-set one- or two-back formation has become a staple lately for teams with great running backs as it allows them to adapt to the play as it emerges.

You can see that coaches have a great many options from which to choose in developing a running attack. They can't have it all. Each coach must choose whether to emphasize a power, quickness, or finesse attack. The coach must then decide whether he or she is going to feature one primary ballcarrier or spread the ball-carrying responsibilities around and balance his attack. He must decide whether to fit the players to his system (making small changes each year to accommodate the abilities of his players) or fit a system to his players—possibly making great changes every year or so. In doing this he might emphasize a tough fullback one year and a fast halfback the next.

CHAPTER 7
Passing Theory

The forward pass is the heart of the pro attack and the delight of the fans. This present-day phenomenon was once a lowly orphan in the game. It wasn't even legal until 36 years after the game was invented. It is an essential part of any offensive plan of attack. While the running game allows the offense to attack the width of the field, the passing game allows the offense to attack both the width and the depth of field.

A great passing attack starts with the offensive line. If the quarterback is about to be sacked or doesn't have time to read the defense, you are not going to have a successful play. The receiver must also have time to run the proper distance. Receivers are generally considered to be the second most important players, while the passer may be the least important. Of course you need all three, but a potentially great passer isn't going to be worth much without receivers who can get open and catch and a line that can protect him.

Teams using the forward pass want to "stretch" the defense vertically and horizontally. They want to be able to hit "out" patterns right on the sidelines (a horizontal stretch), and they want to be able to throw the 60-yard pass deep (a vertical stretch). Once they have established that they can do both of these, the defensive team must be prepared to defend the whole field.

While the Great Wall of China or the Maginot Line of France might well have stopped an infantry and cavalry in their days, neither would be able to stop today's air forces or helicopter warfare. In modern football, one must be able to attack wherever a weakness is found—and weaknesses are often found in the defensive secondary because there is so much field and so few defenders.

For a few teams the pass is primary. Brigham Young University under Lavelle Edwards achieved a great deal of fame and a national title by subscribing to this theory. The San Diego Chargers under Don Coryell and the "West Coast" offense of Bill Walsh's San Francisco 49ers certainly brought the pass into more prominence than it had previously enjoyed. Mike Leach of Texas Tech is the current passing genius. One coach might emphasize the short pass, like Walsh, another might favor the long and intermediate pass, like the Raiders in their heyday. One might emphasize elaborate pass patterns, while another might prefer the passer and receivers "reading" the movements of the defenders before making their final cuts.

The Action of the Passer

The most common type of pass is the "drop back" pass. Drop back passes are designed for the quarterback to drop one, three, five, seven, and sometimes nine steps before firing the ball off toward his receiver. The quarterback's depth depends on the depth that the receiver is to run in his route.

Most teams will also use play-action passes. In this type of pass the quarterback first fakes a running play, then sets to pass. This action usually holds the linebackers and opens up the underneath zones effectively. If the line blocks aggressively as they would do on a running play, the defensive backs may also be fooled. This aggressive blocking may not be able to give the quarterback effective protection. But if they do their normal pass protection blocking (standing up and retreating), it will generally not fool the defensive backs.

Other actions include a rollout, sprint out, partial roll, waggle, and bootleg. In a rollout the quarterback runs wide and deep behind the protection of his backs. This rolling action puts a great deal of pressure on the defensive player who is assigned to cover the short wide area and to support on a wide running play. If the defender drops to protect for the pass, the quarterback may be able to run; if the defender comes up to support the run, the pass is open. A sprint out is faster and shallower. The sprint out is similar to the option play, but while in the option play the quarterback can run or pitch back, in the sprint out he can run or pitch forward. The bootleg is like a rollout, but it is away from the flow of the backs. The quarterback will fake to a back and keep the ball, going in the opposite direction. He may or may not have a pulling lineman to block for him. This play is highly effective on the goal line or in short-yardage situations in which everybody but the quarterback has a man assigned to guard him. A waggle can be a short bootleg or rollout action.

Boot or bootleg: Quarterback fakes one way to backs while he goes the opposite way to run or pass.

Flow: The apparent direction of the ball during a scrimmage play. Most plays attack in the direction of the flow. Counters, reverses, and throwback passes go against the flow.

Waggle: A pass action off a running play in which the quarterback moves wide and deep after faking to a back. Some coaches call it a waggle if the quarterback moves in the direction of the flow behind the backs to whom he has faked. Others call it a waggle if he moves opposite the flow and is protected by a pulling lineman. Most would call this a bootleg.

Rollout: A deep, generally wide path of the quarterback behind the other backs.

Protecting the Passer

There is no question that you can't have a good passing attack unless the passer can release his pass. The more time he has, the more effective he will probably be. Consequently, the blocking schemes that an offensive line must learn in a sophisticated passing attack are quite complicated. The common methods are man, zone, and slide protections. "Big on big" is a commonly used man scheme. If there is a four- or five-man defensive line, the center, guards, and tackles will be responsible for those linemen. Generally the backs will be assigned to block if they see the linebackers rushing, but they may be allowed to swing to the outside if the linebackers drop back.

In order to take away the advantage of the defenders switching positions in a blitz, a "zone" blocking scheme will be used. In a zone scheme the blocker sets up and waits to see who comes into his area. It might be the man who lined up on him, but it might well be somebody else.

Pass Patterns

Pass patterns can be individual routes or team patterns. They may have names or numbers. Most coaches will develop a "passing tree" in which the most common patterns are numbered. Commonly the patterns of the past were designed to break from the line of scrimmage, at 5 yards, or at 10 yards. But as coaches have become more adept at designing patterns to beat where the defenders are more likely to be, the depth of the patterns has changed.

In high school most linebackers are taught to drop back to a 10-yard depth. Consequently passing coaches often have their patterns break at 7 yards (in front of the backers), at 13 yards (just behind the backers, where the receivers can easily slide between the backers), and at 18 yards (safely behind the backers). At the college and professional levels, the routes may break deeper than 20 yards. The types of patterns that the coach will choose to run will be determined by the expected defenses. Theoretically there are six short zones and three deep zones. But no coach is going to consistently commit nine players to these zones and rush only two defenders, so we commonly think in terms of three deep and four shallow zones or two deep and five shallow zones. Defensive coaches will continually change the zones they are protecting and their man-to-man defenses.

Calling the Routes

Pass patterns may have names that describe their actions. A "flag" or "corner" route has the receiver going deep and out toward the marker (which used to be a flag) at the front corner of the end zone. A "post" goes long and in—toward the goalposts. A "buttonhook" or "hook" pattern looks like a buttonhook when drawn on the blackboard. A "spot" pass has the receiver staying in the same spot where he lined up. And an "out" or "sideline" pattern has the receiver going downfield then toward the sideline—and usually coming back slightly toward the line of scrimmage to get away from the defensive back.

As more patterns were developed and passing offenses became more sophisticated, many coaches numbered the patterns. If the patterns were overlaid upon each other they looked something like a tree. By using numbers in progression of short to long passes the coaches could more easily teach more patterns. Assuming that the coach is using the "passing tree" numbers, he might call the split end (usually called the X receiver), the tight end (the Y man), or the flanker or slot (the Z man) as the primary pass receiver. The other receivers might run "complementary" patterns.

For example, if the coach called a "Y 9" or a "Y corner," the tight end would run a corner pattern and the other two receivers should know which complementary patterns to run. Perhaps the nearest other receiver knows that he should run an intermediate level (15- to 22-yard) pattern in the same line of sight as the Y receiver, and the other receiver might have been coached to run a short pattern in the line-of-sight area. This would create a vertical stretch on the defense. If the defense was in typical zone coverage, the Y end should have the deep zone person near him. The second receiver would probably be in the deep curl or "out" area, 15 to 20 yards deep and behind the flat zone cover man. The other receiver would be between the line of scrimmage and five to seven yards downfield, in front of the flat cover man.

 Vertical stretch: Forcing the pass defenders to cover deep even if the pass is in the short or intermediate zones.

A horizontal stretch could be accomplished with four receivers hooking at 8 to 10 yards or curling at 15 to 18 yards and working between the underneath cover men. It could also be done with one or two receivers going deep, then three others running short patterns to one side of the field. The stretch doesn't have to be all the way across the field but can stretch just half of the field. For it to be effective, there must be more receivers in the under zones than there are defenders.

Obviously some patterns work better against some defenses. A fast halfback has the advantage over a slower linebacker if the coverage is man-to-man.

Deep curl patterns (at 18 to 23 yards) would work against most zone coverages. And sending three players deep against a two-deep zone may work. But since coverages are generally disguised, the offensive team is never quite sure what defense will develop as the quarterback drops to pass.

Team patterns are also often called to put some special pressure on the defense. For instance, in a "flood" pattern the offense tries to flood one area with more receivers than can be covered by the defense.

Getting the Receiver Open

If the receiver is being bumped by a defender, he must use a release move. He may use a head fake, fake a block on the defender and then get into his pattern, spin away from the defender, or use his arms to knock the arms of the defender away.

Some coaches teach a hard 90-degree angle cut. A receiver who wants to cut right will plant his left foot and drive hard to the right. Sometimes, especially on deeper routes, the receiver will make a double cut. However, if the receiver can get close to the defender and make the defender turn and run with him, then make his cut when the defender has his legs crossed or his shoulders turned, he can increase the distance between himself and the defender.

Making good cuts (and making them at the proper time) is particularly important in man-to-man coverage. If a team is playing a zone defense, the defenders should be paying more attention to being in the proper place on the field in relation to the ball than to the cut of the receivers. So receivers are often less concerned about faking a defender than they are about getting to an open area between the zones.

Some coaches will not worry so much about making a perfect cut but will tell the receiver the area that they want him in. The passing tree can be used to call this area. The receiver is then taught to recognize man or zone cover as he comes off the line. The defender will generally watch the receiver in man coverage or the passer if he is in a zone, or he will obviously be near his man in man coverage but dropping to an area in zone. If the receiver finds man coverage, he will make a double cut, approach or bump the defender and then break away, or run deeper and then come back. If it is a pure zone cover he merely finds the open area—over, under the cover man, or between the cover people.

Short Passing Game

Short passes are safer. With a one- or three-step drop there is much less likelihood of a sack. The strong, athletic defensive pass rushers have less chance to get to the quarterback. Longer passes are also more likely to be intercepted. At the pro level interceptions are down to their lowest level since 1970, fewer than three a game. Still the average gain per pass is about 11 yards, six on the completion and five on the run after the catch. Because of these factors the vertical game is less important.

CHAPTER 8
Defensive Theory

Most successful coaches believe that defense is the key to winning at any level of play. "You win with defense" is a common axiom in the coaching profession. So while the young coach is spending more time drawing Os for the offensive plays, the wizened old coach is usually playing with the defensive Xs.

With equal material a team should ideally be able to stop the 11 offensive players with 13 to 17 men. If the defense could run a gap eight alignment—a defensive lineman in each of the gaps in the offensive line—to stop the run and had defenders in all six short zones and in all of the three-deep passing zones, the offense would be hard put to move the ball. Unfortunately for defensive coordinators, the rules committee still only allows 11 men on each side of the ball. So the problem is how to get the maximum running and passing defense with only 11 players.

The offense has many advantages over the defense. It knows whether the play will be a run or a pass. It knows the point of attack, and it knows the snap count. In the old days the defenders' major advantage was that they were able to use their hands and arms much more than the offensive players could. Under the current rules the offensive blockers are allowed to extend their hands in blocking, and a great deal of holding is the result. This severely reduces what little advantage the defenders used to have.

A defensive restriction that hurts the pros is not being able to bump pass defenders once they have passed beyond five yards from the line of scrimmage. High school and college defenders are still allowed to bump offensive players as long as they are potential blockers and the pass hasn't been thrown.

With the rules, especially the professional rules, favoring the offense it is much more difficult to field an effective defense. Still there is the burning desire of the defensive coordinators and the defensive team members to hold their opponents scoreless. To do this the defenders must first stop the run. Will they neutralize the blocker and then pursue—the "bend but don't break" idea—or will they attack the offense? Attacking is coming back in style because it also gives the defensive linemen a jump on the pass rush.

Defensive linemen must stop the run in their areas of responsibility, then pursue the ballcarrier if the play is in another area. They must be ready to rush the passer aggressively, but they must still react to the draw play or the screen pass. The linebackers must stop the run, yet they must be able to react to their zones if a pass develops. Defensive backs must stop all the long and short pass patterns while still helping to make tackles on running plays.

In order for a defensive team to hope to stop an offensive team, it must be in an effective alignment, use the proper keys to get the defenders to the right spot, and have techniques that will allow these duties to be accomplished.

Defensive Alignments

Early defensive teams generally used eight people near the ball and three defensive backs. So a six-man defensive line with two linebackers, a "six-two," or a "five-three" alignment, five defensive linemen and three linebackers, was common. As the option play and the passing offense became more productive, teams went to four defensive backs. So with seven men to play linemen or linebackers, the common alignments were four-three or three-four. Steve Owens of the New York Giants is credited with being the first to use the "umbrella" defense with four defensive backs. With a run to one side, the defensive backs could rotate up and still be in a three-deep secondary.

Using four defensive backs made it easier to vary the coverage, changing the zones that each defender covered, and also made it easier to play man-to-man pass defense. It also made it easier to adjust the defense to the offensive strength. If a team came out in a winged formation, all that an umbrella defense had to do was rotate, with a cornerback becoming a defensive end. An eight-man-front team would have to adjust linemen and/or backers to meet that offensive strength.

> *Front:* The alignment of the defensive linemen and linebackers.

With the soundness of the four-deep backs proven, Earl "Greasy" Neale of the Philadelphia Eagles developed a new alignment, still called the Eagle. He used a middle guard who was tough enough to stop up the inside yet could still pursue the ball. His tackles took the guard-tackle gap, often crashing down to stop the trap play. The ends could crash down to stop the off tackle play. The linebackers played on the ends, so they had a good tip on whether the play was a run at them or a pass or run to the opposite side. (If the end released into the secondary, it was a pass or a run the other way.)

This was the forerunner of the modern pro four-three defense. The thinking was that if you wanted the tackles to crash to the guards, why not put them there initially. If the ends were assigned to get to the "off tackle" area, why not put them there first. And if the middle guard (often called "Mike" for "middle in" or "nose man") was to pursue the play, why not move him back to a line-backer spot.

> *Mike:* Middle guard or nose man (Mike means "middle in"), the term used by many coaches to name the middle linebacker.
>
> *Noseguard or nose tackle:* A defensive lineman playing on the offensive center.

Defensive Line Theory

Some coaches want the defender to control the man in front of him. If he can do this, he will be able to control the gaps on each side of him. With the skill and the size of today's offensive linemen, it is often difficult to totally control a man and both gaps. Consequently most coaches have changed their defensive theory to that of "gap control." In a gap control defense the defender may still play on an offensive lineman, but he has primary responsibility for only one of the gaps.

Some coaches just call defenses by designations such as Okie, Eagle, five-three, and so on. The defenders know exactly where to line up for each defense. To upset the offense, the team might "overshift" its line a man or a half a man to the strong side of the formation. When doing this, the linebackers would generally shift the other way so that the defense is still balanced.

Overshift: The alignment of the defensive linemen one man closer to the strength of the formation.

Strong side: The side of the offensive line that blocks for the power plays. Usually the side of the tight end is designated the strong side.

Some years ago Bear Bryant at Alabama popularized the "numbers" defense. This allowed for a great deal of variation in calling defenses. By calling a number the player knew where to line up and what technique to play. The 0, 2, 4, and 6 techniques are head up on the offensive linemen by the nose guard, tackle, and end. The 1 and 7 techniques are inside gap control techniques used by the defensive tackle and end. And the 3, 5, and 9 techniques are outside gap control techniques used by the tackle and end. The 8 technique is that of a wider defensive end. By calling two appropriate numbers the linebacker can align the linemen on his side of the ball in many different spots. The linebacker then goes to the appropriate spot. In coaching clinics today it is universal to use these numbers to designate the lineman's technique.

Techniques of Line Play

Some coaches believe in constantly attacking the offense with their defense. In this scheme the defensive linemen will either charge through an offensive lineman or through a gap in the line. Blitzing teams use this technique with their linemen and their linebackers. Of course there are also many other techniques in the defensive coordinator's arsenal that he can employ.

A "slant" charge is used to move from a man to a gap or from a gap into a man. It changes the attacking point one half man. A "loop" is used to move from one man to another or from one gap to another gap. It moves the attacking point at least one man away from where the defender originally lined up. A team may align in one defense, then all slant or loop to one side or the other. They might be instructed to slant to the strong side of the formation or to the wide side of the field.

Loop: A defensive lineman's move from a gap to a gap or a man to a man.

The advantages of the penetrating defense are that if the defenders guess right they will be at the point of attack and can drop the runner for a loss. Also, if a pass develops, the defensive linemen are already in their pass rush and gain a few steps over where they would have been if they were "reading" the offensive linemen. The disadvantages are that if the play moves away from the penetrating defensive lineman, he is not in a good position to pursue it, so the play might break for a long gain.

The simplest "read" for a defensive lineman is to read the offensive blocker's head. If the blocker puts his head on the defender's right side it is obvious that he is trying to block the defender away from the play, which must be going to the defender's right. So by using a forearm rip or a hand "shiver" the defender should be able to free himself from the blocker, move "across his face," and then make the tackle. In this technique it is essential that the defender not go behind the blocker or he will not be able to pursue quickly. By going behind the blocker he would be screened off from the ballcarrier's path; by staying on the defensive side of the blocker he can take a shorter path to where the ballcarrier will cross the line of scrimmage.

Stunting

As you can imagine, defensive coaches were not content to let their defensive linemen stand like mannequins or blocking dummies, always in the same place. Slanting a lineman into a gap in the offensive line made it more difficult for the blocker to effectively block him. But it left a gap in the defensive line. So coaches ran a linebacker into this gap and transformed a weakness into a strength. It could create a defensive weakness if the play called was a quick pass into that linebacker's zone. But it was a strength if the linebacker could tackle the passer before he threw, or if he tackled a runner before he reached the line of scrimmage. This combination of defensive lineman and linebacker movements is called stunting.

Stunt: A defensive maneuver in which linemen create a hole for a backer to move through the line or a movement between defensive linemen that will allow at least one to penetrate the line of scrimmage.

The Blitz

Stunting of linebackers in pass situations has been around forever. But blitzing corners, strong safeties, and even free safeties are relative newcomers to the defensive arsenal.

At the pro level the blitz is one of the biggest troublemakers an offensive coordinator can encounter. Originally blitzes were packaged with man-to-man coverage. Knowing this, the blitz became easy to attack. So the zone blitz was developed. Since the blitz is designed to get to the quarterback quickly by sending more people to an area than can be blocked, the passer and receivers must be able to recognize the blitz and the coverage instantly to be able to attack it.

Linebacker Play

As mentioned at the start of this chapter, the ideal defense would have at least 17 men on the field—eight linemen and nine pass defenders. Since a team is only allowed 11 men, some must do double duty. The linebackers are the primary double-duty players. They must stop the running play and also defend against the pass. Many plays are designed to force the linebacker into mistakes. The play-action pass, for example, makes the linebacker react to the run while a receiver sneaks into the linebacker's pass zone responsibility. The draw play coaxes the linebacker to drop back. The quarterback drops back as if to pass, and the offensive linemen step back in what appears to be a pass protection block, so the linebacker moves backward into his pass defense zone, but the quarterback hands the ball to a running back so a run comes at him.

The keys that the backers use to react to a run or pass are varied. An outside backer playing on an end may just key his end. If the end releases into the defensive secondary, the backer drops back to his pass defense responsibility. Of course he will need an additional key to make certain that the area he is vacating will not be attacked by a running play—especially a counteraction or a reverse. Inside backers may key the uncovered lineman. The backer can mirror the guards, and if the guards always drop back in pass protection on every pass, and there are no play-action passes, the linebacker should be able to handle both run and pass responsibilities.

Another way that linebackers can cover two areas of responsibility is with controlled stunting. If the running keys are valid, one linebacker may be asked to charge through an opening in the offensive line, known as "scraping" into a gap. The other backer would then be asked to "shuffle" to back up the area vacated by the scraping backer. In order to effectively get the linebackers to react correctly, their keys must be nearly foolproof. Following are some examples of "keys" (looking at only one player) and "reads" (looking at two or more players).

If the attack of the offense doesn't cross its running backs, a key of the near back is the easiest. When a team uses plays in which the backs cross, the key for that game must be the offside back. By keying him, the backer is right whether or not the backs cross. If teams pull their guards in countering actions, such as reverses, the backers will have to read through the guards to the backs. Depending on whether the backs cross or not, the backer's read could be near guard to near back or near guard to far back. If the guard pulls, he becomes the main key; if not, the back is the key.

Defensive Back Play

The defensive back's technique depends on whether he is playing a man-to-man or a zone defense. Generally the back will take a few steps back as he takes his key. A defensive back may key the offside end or the end and tackle.

If both go downfield (in a college or high school game), it is a run or a pass behind the line. (In high school and college linemen can go downfield on passes completed behind the line of scrimmage.) Of course in a pro game the tackle going downfield can only indicate a run because the professional rules do not allow the non-eligible pass receivers to go downfield until the pass is caught.

Zone teams will drop to their zones if a pass shows. They may also rotate their zones if the passer moves to a new position. With teams passing more, especially in certain situations such as third down with five or more yards to go, defensive coaches have begun to put in more defensive backs than the standard four. The five back (nickel defense) and the six back (dime defense) have defensive backs coming in to substitute for linebackers on "passing downs." The advantage of such moves is that the backs have better speed and pass defense skills and are less likely to be "burned" in one-on-one man-to-man coverage against running backs. The disadvantage is that they tend to be weaker against the run than the linebackers, who are typically more powerful, would have been.

Nickel defense: A defense with five defensive backs.

Theories of Secondary Alignment

Coverage players must play pass first. If there is one free safety, he should be in the middle of the field. If there are two deep safeties, they should be about 13 yards in from the sideline. It takes three men to cover the deep secondary zones (zones starting at about 20 yards deep, each being 18 yards wide), therefore many teams use the three-deep secondary—which has been around since the earliest days of the game. Others will rotate or otherwise disguise their intentions of who will be in each zone.

Free safety: The safetyman opposite the power side of the offensive line (the tight end). He is usually free to cover deep zones.

With more teams using two wide receivers, it became impossible to rotate up to stop the run because it would leave the wide receiver unattended. Consequently many teams started to "invert" their safeties. The safeties then became responsible for the run support, while the corners were primarily responsible for the pass.

In man-to-man defense the defenders can play up close and "bump and run" with the receiver. Or they can play "off" their man a bit in "press" coverage, where the defenders take an inside position and get a two- or three-yard head start on the receiver. While there is usually a "free" safety, he cannot cover the whole deep secondary, so the cornerbacks must do most of the job themselves. Teams running the bump and run have the theoretical advantage of being able to take away all of the patterns that the receiver might run. The major disadvantage is that the man covering a wide receiver can't be much help in stopping the running play.

Bump and run: A technique in which the defensive back hits the potential receiver on the line of scrimmage (to slow his route) and then runs with the receiver.

Many teams playing man-to-man defense have their defensive backs start 5 to 10 yards from the receiver. This creates the advantages of being able to take away the long pass with a slower defender and possibly getting some run support from the cornerback. But it has the disadvantage of being open to underneath patterns and to double cutting patterns such as the "out and up" or "hook and go." Double cutting patterns have the receiver making two different moves, such as starting toward the goalpost for a few yards, then cutting to the deep corner of the field, or conversely starting toward the deep corner, then cutting toward the goalposts. It could also be a "stop and go," where the receiver stops, enticing the defensive back to react up, then runs deep behind the defender.

Many teams align four defensive backs across, letting two or three take the deep zones and playing the others in the underneath coverage. As defenses more often face five immediate receivers and more short passes, more variation becomes necessary. But the maxim of taking away the long pass and making the offense go 10 or 12 plays without a penalty or turnover still dominates pass coverage theory.

So you can see there are a lot of possibilities of alignment and of technique. Some teams will use one basic alignment most of the time and will stunt from that set. Other teams will use multiple defensive sets. The important point is really the effectiveness of the individuals playing the defense. How well do they read their keys? How well do they escape their blockers? How well do they pursue to the ballcarrier? How well do they play pass defense?

Defender's-Eye View When Playing in Zone Coverage

The formation and the backfield flow tell how the perimeter of the defense is being manipulated. The wider the wideouts, the wider or deeper the defensive backs must set. If the backs are set wide, there is a greater threat of a swing pass or another type of pass pattern to a back.

What to Watch For

On a pass, the quarterback drops to a spot that should have a direct relation to the depth of the patterns and to the depth the defensive backs should drop.

- Three-step drop. Expect a short pattern in the five-yard area or a timed pattern.

- Five-step drop (about a seven-yard setup). Expect intermediate routes in the 14- to 18-yard area or delayed patterns such as an end dragging or a back out of the backfield.

- Seven-step drop (about a nine-yard setup). Expect deep vertical routes such as streak, post, or corner—or a screen pass.

Knowing the depth of the quarterback's drop should give the defenders an idea of the depth of the pattern. Generally the deeper the quarterback drops, the deeper will be the pass pattern. Then watching the passer's eyes or chin should give an idea of the direction he will throw. It will also give you a hint, as a spectator, of what to look for as you peer downfield.

Drag: A delayed pattern in which a tight end or a wideout runs a shallow pattern across the center.

Streak: A pass pattern in which the receiver runs long and fast.

The most common type of zone coverage is the four-under, three-deep responsibility. Against a team that throws short often, the coach may want to play five-under and two-deep zones. Both defenses may be open to the intermediate area passes of 14 to 18 yards. To take away this intermediate area, the coach may play five-under man-to-man with two-deep zones. This should take away all passes under 18 yards but could be vulnerable to long passes splitting the seams of the two deep safeties. With the under coverage men watching men rather than the ball, this five-under man-to-man defense is vulnerable to the run.

Seams: The areas between the defensive zones, which are more likely to be open to complete passes.

The coach must recognize that there is a defense for whatever the offense wants to do, but every defense has its weaknesses. Because of this, the coach may want to change covers at certain times but not be predictable in so doing. For example, if he plays a five-under man two-deep zone on every third and long situation, his team may be open to a quarterback draw or bootleg or even a sweep into an area being cleared by receivers. The best coaches will always find a way to beat the defense's weaknesses.

CHAPTER 9
Kicking Game Theory

Today, with the emphasis on "special teams," the kicking game has become more important in the eyes of the fans. "Special teams" is the term used for all of the various kicking teams needed during a game: the punt team and the punt block and return team, the kickoff and kickoff receiving teams, the field goal and extra point teams and the field goal defensive team, and the onside kickoff team and the "hands" team that will defend against it. These special teams are made up of members of the offensive and defensive teams with perhaps a few specialists who perform only on the special teams like the kicker or punter. Typically, when fans talk about the kicking game, they think only about the punter or the field goal kicker, but there is far more to the "kicking game" than just the kick. While the fans and some of the commentators lament "the breaks" that lead to a defeat, coaches realize that most of those breaks came from poor coaching or inadequate preparation by one coach or from effective teaching and emphasis by the other coach.

Many of these so-called breaks in a football game occur during the kicking phase of the game. They are not really breaks at all because the "lucky" team has practiced all season to make those "breaks" occur. Bob Shoup, former NAIA national champion coach at Cal Lutheran, said that from his experience, in close games the losing team always seems to make at least two more mistakes in the kicking game than the winning team. Those mistakes can include poor snaps, short kicks, ineffective coverage, a poor hold on a field goal attempt, or inadequate protection. These can result in long returns, blocked kicks, wide field goal attempts, a missed extra point, short punts, and so on.

The kicking game incorporates both offensive and defensive aspects. The punt and kickoff are defensive, but the kick returns, the field goal and extra points, as well as the seldom-seen quick kick are thought of as offensive weapons. Statistics indicate that about one in every five plays is a kicking play. How many coaches practice the kicking game 20 percent of the time? In a two-hour practice, that would be 24 minutes. But kicking game plays are generally more important than most other plays in a game. They often involve scoring or big chunks of yardage, so they can have a marked effect on the field position. And they often involve a change in possession.

Here are some interesting statistics on the games won in the kicking game at the different levels. It has been found that nearly 40 percent of high school and college games are won in the kicking game. At the pro level it is about 30 percent, as you don't have as many mistakes because the snappers, holders, and kickers are the best there are because they practice their skills daily. Still punts, kick returns, and field goals are very important. And when the defense does get a block or a long return is reeled off, it often breaks the game open.

At the pro level each team averages punting about five times, has almost five kickoffs, and has the opportunity to return about four kickoffs and two or three punts. In 1969 George Allen emphasized the importance of the kicking game at the professional level when he hired Dick Vermeil as the first special teams coach. Most teams have special teams coaches today. Many believe that you must win two of the three parts of a football game—offense, defense, and kicking—to win the game.

The Kickoff

A coach can reduce his practice time—and his kickoff effectiveness—by merely putting the ball in the middle of the field and having his best kicker kick it straight down the field. This is probably the best strategy if he has a kicker who can put it out of the end zone every time. But since most teams don't have that luxury, there are a number of approaches to the strategy of kicking off.

If the opponents have a great returner, the kicker can kick away from him or perhaps try a low "squib" kick that will bounce along the ground, allowing the cover people to converge before a return can be set up. A squib kick will take those uncontrolled bounces that only a football can take—so watching the receivers attempt to catch it is like watching Elmer Fudd trying to catch Bugs Bunny.

Some teams will kick the ball from a hash mark rather than the middle of the field to reduce the opponent's options for a return. Their thinking is that it will be more difficult for a team to return to the other side of the field. Every step that the ballcarrier takes to the far sideline gives every member of the kicking team one more step into the receiver's territory, and if the receivers return to the side of the kick, the defenders each have less territory to defend.

The onside kick is actually an offensive play because, since the goal is to recover the ball, the team that is kicking is also attacking. It is an essential part of the kickoff play scheme. It does not have to be limited to end-of-the-game situations where the team is trying desperately to get the ball back so that it can score once more and win. It makes more sense in high school to use a surprise onside kick because the ball is kicked from the 40-yard line, so if the receiving team recovers the ball it will be short of the 50-yard line and will still have a long way to go to score. But at the pro and college levels the ball is kicked from the 30, so if the receiving team recovers it is around the offensive 40-yard line, and the receiving team is put in a pretty good position to score. If the kicking team recovers it is a great advantage for it. And in surprise onside kicks, the kicking team's chance of recovering is near 50 percent.

Covering the kickoff is another important consideration. Coverage for every kick will have two men responsible for the outside. There will also be one or two men who act as safeties. The other seven or eight men will attack the ballcarrier in one or two waves, keeping appropriate distances between themselves so the ballcarrier cannot easily go around them or run through a gap in the wave. Some teams will have a couple of "mad dogs" who will sacrifice their bodies as they attempt to break the wedge of blockers who protect the ballcarrier.

Because some teams specifically assign the coverage men to be blocked on the return, many coaches will cross their rushers as they run downfield. (Usually the return team will match the number of men on the kicking team.) This is particularly true of the ends, because many teams will use a trap on the end as part of their blocking scheme. So crossing the end and one or two other men can foul up the blocking assignments of the return team.

Coverage Assignments

The assignments can vary depending on whether the kick is to be deep (right, middle, or left), cross field (possibly a squib), or an onside kick (a straight-ahead dribbler or a high kick to the sideline). A 50- to 55-yard kickoff should have a hang time of at least 3.9 to 4.0 seconds. This should allow the kicking team to run 30 to 35 yards, which should bring them to about the 30. The returner should catch it near the 10 to 15. The first shot at him should be between the 15 and 25, depending on the depth and height of the kick.

Hang time: The amount of time a kick stays in the air.

Adjustments

Every week the coaches must make some adjustments to the various special teams based on their scouting and film analyses. Scouting considerations include the following:

- What is the receiving formation of your opponent?

- Check the numbers—who plays where?

- Which front men are good targets for onside kicks?

- What types of returns do they run?

- If they use a wedge, do they set it in a specific place on the field, or do they move it to the ball, wherever it has been kicked?

- Who is the best return man?

- Where should you kick your deep kicks?

- Should you squib?

- How can your cover people avoid their blockers?

- Can you use your surprise onside kick against them?

Onside kick: A short kickoff that travels at least 10 yards, which can then be recovered by either team.

The Kickoff Return

In receiving the kickoff, coaches must first plan to defend against the possible onside kick. Next the coach must consider how much time to spend on kickoff return plays. The simplest approach is to wedge and try to get the ball out to the 35-yard line. Sometimes it will break for big yardage. There are many ways to score.

 Wedge: A wedge return generally uses four players who position themselves about 10 yards in front of the ballcarrier, and then block straight ahead as they lead the ballcarrier downfield.

Returning the Deep Kickoff

Generally the kickoff can be considered a success for the kickers if they hold the return team inside its own 25-yard line. It is a definite success for the returners if they get the ball to their own 35. Kickoff return strategies can involve a wedge block, cross block, double-team, trap, or the setting up of a wall of blockers to one side of the field. These may be used in combination. There is also the opportunity for special trick plays. There is the reverse, fake reverse, or the long lateral pass, wherein after the play starts one way the ball is suddenly pitched to the other side of the field.

Coaches realize that no other play has the defense so spread across the field. In no other play is the pursuit reduced as effectively. And in no other play can you predict the defensive reactions as well as you can on the kickoff. For teams that have an effective kicking scheme and practice it well, the yardage rewards are greater than in any other play in the offense.

Pursuit: The movement of the defensive players to get them to a spot where they can make the tackle.

The return scheme for most teams is a wedge. It is relatively simple. The timing of the blocks is not a major factor, and when done effectively it has a good chance of getting the team to the 35. While it sometimes scores, it is not generally the best return for scoring. Some coaches will cross block the middle five or six cover people, then form the wedge behind it. Some will start a wedge but trap out behind it. Some teams will use a simple trap on the widest man. Some will work the middle with one to three double-team blocks to open a lane for the returner.

To use these various attacks, the coach must commit sufficient time to practice them. He can then use the return that will most likely work best against each opponent. If the opponent's kickoff team players stay in wide lanes as they cover the kick, a wedge or a series of double-team blocks may work. If most of the coverage people converge on the ball but the widest defenders stay wide, the wide defenders might be blocked out and trapped, and the kick returner can run wider but inside the trapped cover man. For creative coaches, there are lots of possibilities for returning a deep kickoff.

The Punting Game

Most coaches believe that the punt is the single most important play in a game. Some think the punter is the most important man in the equation, some think it is the snapper. Legendary coach Paul "Bear" Bryant estimated that 98 percent of blocked punts occur because of a poor center snap. The long snap requires that the snapper pass the ball quickly to the punter. The snap should take 0.6 to 0.7 second to get the ball back 10 yards, 0.75 second if the punter is 13 yards back, and 0.8 second if the punter is 15 yards back. The punter can kick the ball high and straight, but many coaches today ask their punters to kick directionally, about 10 to 15 yards to one side. This forces the punter to move and brings him closer to a "gunner." Since the object of the punt is to gain as many yards as possible, it is generally not best to kick into the end zone. The pros now keep statistics on how effective their punters are in starting their opponents inside their 20-yard line. To kill the ball inside the 20, kickers will either kick out of bounds or use a "pooch" punt in which the ball is kicked high to about the 10 while the covering team attempts to let the ball bounce toward the goal line but not cross it.

 Punt: A kick made on a scrimmage down that is designed to make the most yardage when possession is changed.

As the coach, you must know the game situation. Where should the punter kick? Out of bounds, wide, to the right or left? What if it is a bad snap? Should the player fall on it or try to kick or run it? If it is a bad snap in the end zone, should you take a safety, thereby giving up two points but gaining the opportunity to rekick from the 20-yard line? Probably if your team is ahead by three or more it is a good idea. Perhaps even if you are only ahead by two—a shot in overtime would certainly be better than giving up a touchdown. Just kicking long is not the answer. A shorter but high kick with no return is generally better than a long kick with an effective return. Kicking into the end zone reduces the net by 20 yards when the ball is brought out to the 20. Such a kick is usually the coach's fault for not teaching the pooch kick and coverage or the out-of-bounds kick. Certainly here we must have a *collective mentality* between the coach, the punter, and the cover people. Coaches must practice every possible situation that might put them over the top. There shouldn't be many times in a game where players are facing a situation that is a total surprise and has not been practiced.

Fake Punt

Of course it takes real courage to run or pass on fourth and 10, but if the odds favor faking a punt, it may be worth a shot. If the coach decides to use the fake punt, the players need to work on it intensely, or they risk failing in the attempt. If a team can run part of its regular offense, with its regular people, as part of its fake punt, it will increase the odds for success.

Fourth-down fake punts can make or break a game. If the play is unsuccessful, the team will have lost the 35 to 40 yards it could have had with a punt. That's a big play going the wrong direction. Certainly nobody is going to be fooled by a fake punt when a team is behind by six with two minutes to go and the ball around the 50. If the players go into punt formation, their opponents will all be yelling, "Watch the fake!"

The teams that have always exploited the fake punt play are those that use their kicking game as an important part of their offense. If they have punted on third down before, the next punt formation on third down will send the safety scurrying back. What a time to hit his vacated area. It doesn't take too much practice to snap to an up back and sweep. If the team has a quarterback as an up back, it can run an option to the punter.

Certainly the punt return team is open to a number of possibilities. Do the linemen hit, then immediately start into their punt return blocking responsibilities? If so, a run nearly anywhere could work. One highly successful high school coach in California allows his punters the option of throwing to a wide end if he is uncovered. It is a play that is practiced often and that makes a good many yards.

Many teams incorporate the fake punt into their punting plans. They don't know when they leave the huddle what their play will be. The deep back will check the defense, then signal by a code word whether to run the fake punt and pass, the fake punt and run, or actually punt the ball. This is one down where a coach has a pretty good idea of the defensive plans—who will be aligned where, whether the defenders are rushing or holding up the cover people, and whether they have one or two safeties deep. There is no defensive situation that allows the offense more options. Of course, again, if the play is unsuccessful, the team will have lost the 30 to 40 yards it could have had with a punt.

Punt Defense—Blocks and Returns

As you can imagine, in defending a punt a team can plan to return it, block it, or use a combination of the two—and it must defend against the fake. This means that the defenders must have assignments for the fake punt and run and for fake punt and pass possibilities. We have all seen punters run, because of either intelligence or fear, and gain an easy first down. So the defensive coach must set players to stop both the wide run and the pass.

The coach's primary thought will probably be to concentrate on either blocking or returning the punt. Some teams try to block nearly every punt. Some teams try to return nearly every punt. Since it is so difficult to block a punt and so easy to rough the punter and be penalized 15 yards and a first down, most teams will opt to return the punt.

Most teams use a 10-man defensive front with a single safety. This 10-man front gives the maximal chance of both blocking the punt and holding up the cover people. If the offensive team splits two ends to release quickly and tackle the punt returner, the defense must split two defenders to hold them up. Many teams are using the pro-style punt with split ends and with wingbacks just outside the offensive tackles. Each of these people must be covered in case of a fake punt and pass. Coaches interested in the full exploitation of the possibilities of the kicking game offense will throw to any of these people if they are uncovered.

The Punt Return

A team attempting to return the punt will generally try to hold up the tacklers on the punting team. With the pros being able to release only the two widest men on the snap of the ball, most pro teams will use two men to hold them up. At the high school and college level, everyone can release, so all potential tacklers should be delayed. For the punt return the team will want to hold up the linemen, particularly the widest cover people. Some teams will only hold up those on the side of the return while getting those on the other side of the line into the wall more quickly.

The longer the team holds the opposition on the line of scrimmage, the greater the opportunity for a successful return. Naturally the coach will always have somebody rush just in case there is a bad snap or a fumble. With a returner and a rusher there are nine other people to hold up the punting team's cover people. What is the best way to do that? If the defenders release too fast to get into the wall, the defense may be setting itself up for a fake punt. More than once a punter has looked at the eager defenders running to set up a wall, then taken the ball and run the other way for big yards. A few years ago in a major Southeast Conference game there was some confusion. When the ball was snapped, the right side of the defense peeled off to the right, the left side peeled off to the left, and nobody rushed the punter. He alertly tucked the ball away and ran right up the middle for a 50-yard touchdown. Only the safety realized that the ball hadn't been kicked!

If the kicker can kick the ball high and get a good "hang time," the tacklers have more chance to cover the punt. Since it takes about two seconds for a kicker to get off his punt and most good punters hang the ball up for about four seconds and kick about 35 to 40 yards, the punt coverage team has about six seconds to cover 35 to 40 yards. And since most special teams players will run a 40-yard dash in less than or near five seconds, there will be no chance for a return unless the coverage people are held up for at least two seconds.

Once the punting team members have escaped the men who were delaying them, the receiving team members will set up for their return. Most teams will form a wall of players on one side of the field. They will generally choose the wide side of the field or a return left against a right-footed kicker. (Generally the ball will drift to the right of a right-footed kicker.) The punt can be considered a success for the punting team if it nets 35 yards. It is a success for the returners if the punt nets less than 25 yards.

Punt Blocking

When a team concentrates on punt blocking, the punting team must hold its blockers in longer, so they are slower in getting downfield to tackle the punt returner. This may be an advantage to the blocking returning team in making successful returns. If it is rushing four people, there are still six who can get into the return after they have performed their first responsibilities as hole openers or to contain people watching for the fake punt. Some teams block lots of punts and field goals. If the head coach can get his fastest and most courageous players in on the punt block and he is willing to dedicate the practice time needed, his team *will* block punts.

Generally the scouting report will play a large part in determining whether to attempt to block the punt. A center who makes slow snaps or who is often inaccurate may issue an invitation to block his team's punt. A kicker who takes too long to get off a punt or who takes more than two steps before kicking is a prime target for a block. And of course there are tactical situations in which a block may be called, such as when behind late in the game or when the opponent is backed up close to his end zone. Scouts will time the punter in the pregame practice and in the game itself to determine whether he is a good candidate for a punt block. They will also note how many yards he covers with his steps so that the punt block spot can be measured exactly.

As an involved spectator, if you have a stopwatch handy, you might time the snapper and punter in their pregame warm-ups and during the game to see if they are slow and whether a punt block might be successful.

Since the ball will generally be kicked from about three to four and a half yards in front of where the kicker started, most punt blockers are told to aim for a spot four and a half to five yards in front of the kicker's starting point and a foot to his right—if he is right-footed. Some coaches are more cautious and set the spot six yards from the place where the punter started. This can reduce the chances of roughing the punter, and if the punt rusher finds he can get the kick you can be sure he will go past that six-yard spot. This is about eight or nine yards behind the center. So the punt blockers have about 1.8 to 2.2 seconds to run 8 to 12 yards—depending on whether they are rushing from the middle or from the end of the defensive line. The team will need two blockers coming free because the personal protector will usually block one of them.

Field Goals and Conversions

There is no question that the abilities of modern kickers have increased the chances of success for a field goal or extra point. About 30 years ago there were fewer than 100 field goals each year in major college football. Today there are hundreds each year. Field goals at the pro level have increased to 3.4 per game, a bit more than 10 points per game. The more productive offenses bring the ball into field goal range more often, and the better kickers are making longer field goals more often. This has great ramifications for coaches' approaches to the field goal, the extra point, and their defense.

The snapper, holder, and kicker are each of critical importance, and each needs to be coached long and hard during the off-season. Then they need to practice daily during the season as well. The snapper must snap the ball back fast and to a point where the holder can get it to the ground quickly. Good snappers also get the laces into the holder's hands so he doesn't have to spin the ball. The holder must get the ball on the ground at the spot where the kicker knows it will be, while turning the laces toward the goalposts. If the laces are not "on center," the kicked ball will drift to the side of the laces. Many kickers' kicks drift to the side of the kicker's follow-through. To avoid this outcome, the holder will tilt the top of the ball away from the projected drift. The time from snap to kick should be 1.4 seconds or less.

Watch the close-up of the holder on TV. If the snapper and holder do their jobs properly, the kick should be automatic. But if the snap is off and delays the hold or the hold is not on the expected spot, the kicker has another variable or two to contend with and his chances of success are reduced.

Defending the Field Goal or Extra Point Attempt

Teams will try to block the field goal or extra point either by attempting to collapse the middle of the offensive line or by overloading at the end of the line. If a team has some very strong linemen who can collapse the offensive middle and a tall jumper or two to bring in behind them, it may have a shot at the middle block. When Ted Hendricks was with the Raiders, the team had much success with this type of block.

The scouting report will be very useful in determining the most obvious weakness in the offensive blockers. The angle of the kick upward is also very important. A kick that rises fast doesn't give as much of a chance for a block, but if the scouting report shows that the kick generally has a low trajectory, the team has a shot at it. Long field goal attempts usually have lower trajectories.

Most teams come off the corner for the block. To do this, one man will occupy the offensive end, another will rush inside the wingback, and a third will rush from outside the wingback. The inside man must shoot close to the tails of the blockers, starting in an almost flat path, then adjust to a spot a yard in front of the ball placement. His flat path behind the end makes it very difficult for the wing to effectively block him while blocking the outside rusher. If he rushed directly at the blocking target, it would be easier for the wing to make contact with both players. He will have to travel about seven yards to the blocking point.

The outside rusher takes a path directly to the spot a yard ahead of the ball placement. He will have to travel about eight yards to the blocking point, but his approach will be a straight line. Can these players run eight yards in 1.3 to 1.5 seconds? If so, they have a shot at blocking the field goal.

Now that you have an idea of the basics of the offensive, defensive, and kicking games, we can go deeper into "the game" to bring you to a more advanced appreciation of what is happening and why.

A Coach's Idea of the Game: Beyond the Xs and Os

Deciding on Plan

Understanding the various theories of offense, defense, and kicking gives you a good start on "unconfusing" the game. But each team's games are a week apart. From high school through the pro level, "the game" takes that whole week. All-time great NFL coach Vince Lombardi said, "Winning isn't everything, but preparing to win is!" During the six days of preparation the coaches watch their own team's game on tape to see where the team needs to improve. They grade each player on every play so they can help the individual players to improve. They watch several of the opponent's games and prepare the scouting report. Then they must plan the practices to work on the things that will prevent their team from losing and the things that will help it to win. Having a plan for victory before the game even begins, and adjusting to the unforeseen, is what coaching is all about.

Since each football team will use basically the same offensive and defensive theories throughout the year, opponents have a pretty good idea of what to expect in terms of formations, basic plays, and basic defensive alignments. Some high schools may scout a team only once, but most high schools, colleges, and the pro teams scout many games. Generally the opponent's last three games and the games the team has played against your team give more than enough information. Scouting these games should give some insight into the opponent's basic theories and strategies, and it gives a pretty good idea of which players will be playing in the game against you.

Developing the Offensive Strategy

Once the tendencies of the defense have been charted, the coach can begin to plan his own strategy of attack. If the opponents have shown marked tendencies against every team they have played, it gives the coach a good hint as to what might work against them:

- Do they have certain tendencies on third and one when the game is tied?

- Do those tendencies change if they are ahead or behind?

- Are they likely to pass from inside their own 20-yard line?

- Do they usually run to the wide side of the field or to the right side of their formation?

- When are they likely to blitz?

- Does the team nearly always stunt in a third and long situation?

- Do they often or always run a man-to-man defense against a short passing offense or when they are in a goal line defense?

- Do they generally slant their defensive linemen to the wide side of the field?

- Do they usually stay in the same pass coverage, or do they vary it?

- What are they likely to do in a third and long situation?

- What is their goal line defense?

- When do they go into their true goal line defense?

These are some of the questions that must be answered if an effective strategy is to be implemented for the next game.

If a team blitzes often and tips it off with the movement of the players, like bringing the backers closer or cheating a cornerback in or up, the quarterback should be taught to recognize the blitz before the snap. He might then be able to change the play, or make an "audible," at the line of scrimmage to capitalize on the weakness of that defense. In addition pass patterns might have to be adjusted in blitz situations. Since a team might run a certain blitz only once or twice during a game, the coach will have to make sure that the quarterback and receivers can recognize special blitzes the instant they are evident.

Not only do all of these decisions have to be made, but they have to be made the day after the most recent game and formulated into a game plan within two days so that the practices can be geared to perfecting the game plan.

Audible: Calling the offensive play at the line of scrimmage.

Strategy to Beat the Defense

Offensive coaches should first try to beat the opponent's basic defensive alignment, its theory of defense, and its basic pass coverage. It is crucial to determine whether the team generally runs a four-three or a three-four, whether the linemen charge hard or play more of a "hit and react" technique, and also whether the defense is primarily a man-to-man or a zone team.

Next the coach must try to create a mismatch. In developing a passing strategy, perhaps the coach can put his best receiver on the opponent's poorest defender. Or if the opposing players run a lot of zone defense, he might try to get two men into one defender's zone. If they play a lot of man-to-man defense, he should try to get the team's fastest receiver on the opponent's slowest defender, such as a running back against a linebacker, then let him run a deep pattern.

In developing a running strategy, the coach might try to create a mismatch by bringing his tight end to the side toward which he wants to run so that he can double-team a tough defensive end. Or he might motion a slot back to help block at a certain hole. Maybe the back could trap a lineman from the outside or perhaps help out on a double-team. If an opponent plays a lot of zone defense and doesn't adjust well to the changed strength of a new formation, the coach might motion a man from one side of the field to the other. He also might motion a flanker to the play side and thus gain an additional blocker. Or, if it is a pass play, he gains an extra receiver, so he may outnumber the pass defenders.

Strategies for Blocking Problem Defenders

At the higher levels of football, many teams like to have at least two ways to block every problem defender. The outstanding players just can't be handled on every play with a one-on-one basic block. They have to be hit by different people, both linemen and backs, and they may have to be double- or triple-teamed if you expect your quarterback to survive until halftime.

 Hall of Fame coach Hank Stram was outstanding on scouting personnel and coming up with ways to beat certain individuals. He would look for the two or three best people on the opposing team, the ones that had to be controlled to win, then devise ways to beat them. He didn't want opposing players or teams to be able to effectively do what they had been able to do best.

Against a quick-reacting linebacker, a coach might run play-action passes to keep the linebacker out of his zone, or a draw play might work if the backer reacts back very quickly to the quarterback's drop. Since the linebackers are so key to both the run defense and the pass defense, coaches continually try to fool them by getting them to be too aggressive rushing on a play-action pass, by being in a pass zone when a delayed run or draw play is called, or by using misdirection, getting the linebacker moving in one direction by the flow of the running backs, then attacking his area with another ballcarrier after he has left to pursue the other running backs.

Against a great defensive back, a coach might swing a back into his area but near the line of scrimmage after sending another receiver deep in his zone. Or maybe the quarterback would "look him off"—look one way to get him moving that way, then quickly throw the other way.

Another way to work on a good defensive lineman who reacts well is to influence him. In an influence block, one man false-blocks a defender, then releases on a linebacker or defensive back. A trapper then comes to take the defender in the same direction he is reacting.

Influence: Getting an opponent to move in the direction desired through finesse.

Running Game Strategy

First the coach must determine whether the opponent's running defense is based on a "hit and pursue" or an "attack and penetrate" type of defense. When playing against the strong pursuit teams, the offense might well think first of quick plays and counterplays. When playing against an attacking defense, the offense might think of using wide plays, especially the quick pitch, and trapping plays.

Next the coach has to look at the basic alignment used by the opponent's defense. How many "down linemen" does the opponent use—three, four, five, or six? Do they stay in that set, or do they over- or undershift it often? (An overshift involves moving the linemen toward the strength of the offensive formation. An undershift involves shifting the linemen away from the strength of the formation.) Since every alignment has its limitations as well as its strengths, the offensive coach must prepare to attack weaknesses in both the alignment and in the individual defensive players.

A prepared coach would also do well to learn whether the opposing team blitzes or stunts. If so, he must find out when is it most likely to do so: on obvious passing downs, on long yardage, on short yardage, on first down. Determining who is most likely to stunt is important too. It could be a middle backer, an outside backer, a safety, or a corner who does it, so it's important for the coach to have an idea of who to anticipate. The defenders might also prefer to "twist" the linemen when rushing a pass, while keeping their backers free to pursue the run or drop for the pass.

 Twist: A movement between defensive linemen, especially in a pass situation, in which the linemen cross hoping that at least one will get clear into the backfield.

What are the linebackers keying on? Do they seem to key the guards, the fullback, the halfback? If so, a false pull and a counter might work. If linemen or backers follow an offensive lineman's pull, they can be blocked from behind by another lineman and the ballcarrier can cut behind the block. Or if the backers are keying the main ballcarrier, the tailback, a countering play using the fullback going in the opposite direction can work. Or both running backs can run in the same direction, but the ball can be given to a receiver running in the opposite direction—a reverse or an "end around."

The opposing team might also pursue too quickly. Recently a pro team that didn't run many reverses was playing against a team that pursued very quickly. For that week the team worked on a reverse. When it used the play the following week, it scored. The next week, knowing that the opponents knew about the reverse, the team faked the reverse and threw a pass for a touchdown. This strategy shows the coach's awareness of scouting in the NFL. He knew the other team would be expecting the reverse, and so he capitalized on it.

The coach must keep an eye on the defensive backs, too. If the opponent is a four-deep team, it might get its run support mainly from the safeties or from the corners. Does it play a lot of man-to-man? If this is the case, perhaps a wide run at a cornerback who is retreating and watching his man run deep, rather than watching for the run, might be successful.

The offensive strategist must also look for weaknesses in the individual linemen and linebackers. Injured starters might be replaced by far less capable or more inexperienced players, which might give the other team an advantage. A player might be adept at going to his right but not his left, a flaw that a savvy coach should be able to exploit. A linebacker might react too slowly to a run or commit so quickly that he might be vulnerable to a play-action pass, a counter, or a special blocking technique.

Sometimes a coach can predict, nearly without error, what a team will do in a highly specific situation. Several years ago in a playoff game the Raiders' coaches were nearly certain that the Broncos would use a specific defense on a third and one situation, and they prepared a play that they were 98 percent certain would score against this defense. The team never got into a third and one situation in the game, but if it had occurred the players would have been ready with this piece of strategy.

Some years ago the Raiders decided to use the halfback pass against Seattle. Marcus Allen was a quarterback in high school, so he threw a pretty good pass. They waited for a short-yardage situation, then tossed to Marcus, who was running wide. He pulled up and threw a pass for a touchdown. A few weeks later, against the Chargers, the play was used again, this time for 40 yards and a score. So the coaching staff decided that they needed this play in their offense. While it was put in originally as a "big play" for a specific game, it became an integral part of the offense and kept the defensive backs from coming up too soon to stop the run. The threat of the pass made the run more effective.

Developing the Passing Strategy

Some teams, such as the Raiders, always want the threat of the deep pass. If it's there—great! If not, it opens up other things, like 20-yard curls or outs. Often those 20-yard patterns go all the way.

When a coach expects a defensive line to hit and pursue on the run, he can expect a somewhat slower pass rush because the defender must first hit, then recognize the pass, then rush. This is slower than the defender who is aggressively attacking a gap. In order to combat the hard-charging linemen and the blitzing defenses, a coach might decide to just throw short. This is what Miami did in beating the "bad Bears" of 1985. Instead of having the quarterback drop seven steps, he might just use the patterns that have one-, three-, or five-step drops with quick releases. Or if the coach has a mobile quarterback, he may have the passer sprint or roll away from the rush.

The offensive coach must also account for every possible rusher on or near the line of scrimmage. At the more advanced levels of football, the offense should have more than one way to block each of these defenders. If the defense is overloaded to one side, the linemen should be able to slide over to pick up the possible rushers, the tight end might shift over to the defensive strong side, or the coach could have a back ready to block to the side that the defense has overloaded.

While a "big play" team may actually call only six or eight long passes in which the deep man is the prime receiver, it will have potential receivers running deep patterns quite often—even if the quarterback isn't paying any attention to them.

Developing the Overall Game Strategy: The Game Plan

In preparing for a team, we coaches have to think of the overall theories of the opposing coach. What does he like to do? Is he conservative, or is he a gambler? If he has been in the league a long time, the other coaches know a lot about him. But what about the new coach in the league? Since the head coach is primarily responsible for the overall offensive and defensive strategy, it is imperative to be able to "get into his head" when making the game plan. You are looking for the odds to be changed in your favor by correctly analyzing what a team has done, when they have done it, and whether they can do it against you next week.

One concern always on a coach's mind in planning for a game is the question of how to win the takeaway battle. When watching a game, can you spot some ways to steal the ball from a passer or ballcarrier? Does the quarterback hold his arms wide when he drops back to pass? If so, the opponent can work on a blindside strip with the blitzer driving his hands inside the passer's elbows and ripping down. Does a ballcarrier always carry the ball in his right arm? Then when he runs to an opponent's right the player has a better chance for a strip.

A team can't change its overall style every week and still be successful. Since the execution of the plays is of critical importance, new plays, pass patterns, defensive reads, or pass coverages can't be introduced on a weekly basis. However, a coach may change something just a bit. He might decide to run a pattern a few yards deeper than normal or throw the halfback pass to a different player or from a different formation. It may be just enough to throw off the opponents but not enough to take a lot of practice time to perfect.

Most coaches will call certain plays early in the game to see how the defense will adjust. Years ago Sid Gilman, one of the finest coaches the game has ever seen, got credit for using the first quarter to analyze the opponent's defense—then attacking that defense for the next three quarters. Special preparation is needed for third and three, third and short, short-yardage passes, red zone offense (from the 20- to 25-yard line—the red zone may vary week to week), from the 10 to the 3 or 4, from the four-yard line to the goal line. These are critical situations because the team must win the third-down situation to get a new first down, and near the goal line it must score. Football is a game of varying situations. Coaches must plan for the major situations that may occur. Most coaches develop a "ready list" of plays for each situation. Both the head coach on the field and the offensive coordinator in the press box will have copies of this list.

Developing the Defensive Strategy

The coach's first consideration is to take away the opposition's bread-and-butter plays, whether it is the off tackle, the isolation series, or the short passing game. He must stop what the opposing players do best and get them to try to beat his team with their secondary attack. Next he wants to know when his team might get a big defensive play. The coach should go for the big defensive play when the opponents have been forced into an obvious passing situation. If he can get a sack at this time, the opponents lose a lot of yardage and their down. In these situations it's worth it to take a gamble to get the "big play." It's not like Las Vegas. A coach should always gamble when the odds are in his favor. If a coach is going to play the pass line, he wants the dice loaded!

Defensive Strategies in Special Situations

Against a team with one outstanding receiver, a coach might decide to double cover him all the time or perhaps only in certain passing situations. A coach might also just use his best defender to cover the outstanding receiver if the player is skilled enough to do so. Sometimes it's not just a player on the opposition that merits a defensive adjustment—sometimes it will be the team's tactics. Against a team with a good short passing attack, a coach might decide to go man-to-man often. While a zone defense is usually more effective against the long and intermediate passes, it tends to be weaker against the short passing attack.

In looking at the scouting reports, it may be revealed that a team has pet formations for favorite plays. Or the team may use its motion back extensively—using him to lead block or trap when he is near the offensive line and using him as a prime receiver when he is wider. If so, he becomes a major key for the defense. Or the opponent may ignore its back in motion, using him only to shift or spread the defense. During the week's practice sessions, recognition of the opponent's formations and plays is the major defensive concern. It may change the defense when a formation or motion occurs. Perhaps an automatic stunt or blitz, or a change in the pass coverage, will be signaled when a tendency is recognized.

The scouting report may reveal that the team plays very conservatively inside its own 30. This means that the defense can become more aggressive and perhaps downplay the possibility of a pass. The report may show that the team favors running to the wide side of the field. This could signal the defensive coordinator to slant the line or stunt a linebacker into the expected flow of the play.

Perhaps the linebackers have been taught to key the guards, but the opponents never pull the guards or double-team with them—so a better key might be found for that game.

Sometimes the scouts will pick up a "cheat" that can be exploited by the defense. A fullback might line up closer than normal on cross bucks or when he is expected to pass block. Or maybe a flanker will line up closer to the center if he is going to run a reverse. Or a tight end might cheat out a bit when he is going to release for a pass.

One major point is that a team should not be predictable on offense or defense. Smart coaches will pick up these tendencies and beat the team with them.

Kicking Game Strategy

The kicking game is a highly scouted aspect of football. It is an area in which many "breaks" can be made, especially if they are planned.

Among the things that are considered when the other team is kicking off are the average distance of the team's kicks, the average hang time, the type of kick coverage, and the speed of the kickoff team. If the opponent's kickoff is generally short, a coach may emphasize the return that week. If the kicking team coverage players stay in lanes like they are supposed to do (about three to five yards apart), a middle return will probably work best. If they converge quickly on the ball, a wide return may be best. If most of them converge but those responsible for the wide plays stay wide, then a trap return will probably work best. If the kicking team crosses its widest men to make it more difficult to trap, that has to be taken into consideration in setting up the blocking rules. If the other team peels back quickly on the kickoff, he might consider an "onside" kickoff.

When his team is kicking, a coach must consider which player is the opponents' best return man and kick away from him. He must know if the opposing players are likely to wedge, cross block, or trap in order to prepare the coverage people for blocks from the side or blocks from the front such as occur in a wedge return.

As discussed in the previous chapter, when the other team is punting it's important to know how many seconds it takes for the center to snap the ball to the kicker and how long it takes the punter to get the ball off. (Taking more than 2.2 seconds is usually a signal that the punt can be blocked.) Does the punter take long steps? Is the center likely to snap high or on the ground? If so, it's a good opportunity for a block.

The coach will have to decide where the block should occur. Usually the blockers aim five yards in front of the spot where the kicker lined up, but if the punter takes short steps the target for the block might be at four yards. Next the coach will have to determine where to attempt the block. Are the opposing linemen tightly spaced? If so, the players might be able to block from the outside. Or are their gaps wide enough that an inside stunt might work?

The punting team surely wants to make certain that it gets the punt off. But if the opposing team never rushes the punter, a coach might think of having the punter hold the ball for a second before he kicks it to give his coverage people a chance to get farther downfield. If the return team players hit and peel back to set up a return, the kicker might fake the punt and pass or run.

In the 1966 Rose Bowl, UCLA pulled off what might have been the biggest upset in this traditional game. Top-ranked, undefeated Michigan State was favored by two touchdowns. After a fumbled punt, UCLA scored. They kicked onside and recovered, then quickly marched 42 yards to score. The Bruins got all of their 14 points without the Spartans touching the ball. Then they held on to win 14–12. Tommy Prothro, the UCLA coach, was a championship bridge player as well as a successful coach. His strategic and tactical decisions won a good many games for him—at the card table and on the gridiron.

The Challenge of Making Strategic Decisions

Some teams stay very basic with their offense and defense. Their idea is to minimize their own mistakes. Other teams look for technical advantages and change somewhat from week to week in their attack and defense. Sometimes the strategy hinges on pregame publicity. In 1904 Coach Fielding Yost at Michigan publicized the fact that his 265-pound lineman, Babe Carter, would carry the ball near the goal line. In the game he inserted Carter as a back when his team got near the goal line. Carter faked, and another back scored.

The hype of the 1986 Super Bowl had many people wondering. Would Tony Eason be able to play even though he had the flu? Or would Steve Grogan start for New England? Would McMahon be able to play with his sore buttock, or would his acupuncturist have to start the game instead? A defense might prepare somewhat differently depending on which quarterback might start, so the supposed pregame indecision by one coach might result in a lot of headaches for his opponent. The Terrell Owens injury before the 2005 Super Bowl also had people wondering. Of course Terrell said he would play—and he did.

Before their playoff game meeting in 1986, John Robinson of the Rams said that Dallas would often add plays if there was a strategic reason for it, but the Rams were not inclined to do anything different from week to week. Then in the game it was the Rams who had all the new plays.

The coaching staff will generally see more things that they could do than the team will have time to practice. The major question is whether the time spent in teaching the changes in offense, defense, or kicking will gain more than spending time polishing the basic plays and defenses. For many coaches, the week-to-week strategic adjustments are the most interesting and challenging aspects of the season. This is, perhaps, the major factor in the "violent chess match" of football.

Most coaching staffs will not go "out of character" for a big play. They won't change a basic run or pass play just to gain a small advantage, because the practice time it would take to perfect the changes would not be worth the expected result. When they do make changes, it is more likely to be in the passing game than in the running attack, because passing changes are easier to install. Passes usually involve only two or three people, while a running change would require the whole offensive unit to be involved in the learning process.

Defensively, coaches have to be prepared not only for what opponents have done but for what the opponents might do. The "what if" part of the preparation can drive a coach crazy. "What if" they have their reverse man throw a pass? "What if" they run a hook and lateral? "What if" they try a reverse on the kickoff?

To effectively plan the strategy for the next game, a coach must understand the mentality of his opponents. Why do they use a certain formation? Why do they use a certain personnel grouping? What are they thinking in each down and distance situation when tied, ahead, behind? Why do they use motion or shifting? When behind late in the half or at the end of a game, does their mentality change? Each answer to these questions signals an adjustment in the defensive strategy.

Any of these strategic decisions may be overruled by the tactical situations that occur during the game. Perhaps the wind is blowing so hard that it is impossible to pass. Or maybe the fog arrives and makes it impossible to pass long, so the defensive backs can be moved up. Perhaps there is an injury to the team's best receiver. These and many other possible situations can alter the pregame strategy and require a tactical adjustment.

In 1985 San Diego Charger coach Don Coryell installed the power I as part of his offense. It was a formation he had used as a college coach at Whittier. Don was hard enough to prepare against with his helter-skelter offense, then he put in this power attack. The Raiders made adjustments during the week, but Coryell added some motion and some other formation changes that weren't expected. The Raiders' "what if" preparation wasn't complete. They lost in overtime 40–34.

CHAPTER 11

Tactics: Making Adjustments During the Game

◆◆◆◆◆◆◆◆◆◆◆◆◆◆◆◆◆◆◆◆◆◆◆◆◆◆◆◆◆◆◆◆◆◆◆◆

Perhaps the toughest part of coaching is making the tactical adjustments that are necessary during a game. Seeing an unexpected defense; a substitute starting in place of a regular; being hurt by new plays, different formations, or new types of motion—all can force quick adjustments in the game. Also seeing how the opponents adjust to a team's tactics can force some quick thinking on the part of the coach. The major point is, *don't panic.*

Intelligent tactical decisions play the percentages. Going for a first down on fourth and two on your opponent's 45 is generally not as good a percentage play as a punt. However if it is late in the game and you are behind, your chances of winning are much better if you try for the first down.

Another tactical concern is the emotional factor. This is a reason that coaches will often go for the "sure" field goal on fourth and one on the one-yard line. If the defenders hold you scoreless they get highly confident and the offense feels bad. Even a field goal will make the offense feel superior and the defense feel that it has failed.

Tactical Adjustments on Offense

At the professional level some of the tactics relate to making substitutions based on the other team's subs. Most teams do this. While in the huddle the linemen will peek at the incoming subs and alert the quarterback to a possible audible call. One time when Dallas played the Bears, every time Dallas sent in seven defensive backs on third and long, Mike Ditka called for a draw type of play. When the Cowboys made their adjustment and started going for the running back, the quarterback faked the draw and threw long to set up a key touchdown.

Historically Speaking

Some years ago, Kansas City planned to stop the Raiders' running attack with five defensive linemen rather than their normal four-man front. It took the Raiders by surprise, but they soon realized that in playing a five-two alignment up front the Chiefs would have to play man-to-man in the secondary. The Raiders split Cliff Branch as an end and put one back outside the tackles in a double wing. This forced the Chief safeties to "lock up" on the wingbacks and left no free safety to help on Branch. He faked out and went to the post, which, of course, was wide open. The 50-yard touchdown forced the Chiefs out of their five-man line and allowed the Raiders to revert to their game plan, which was primarily a running attack.

What are the opponents doing on passing downs? Are they using five or six defensive backs—a nickel or dime defense? Do they change from situation to situation? One successful professional team will often try for a sack on second and long yardage by playing a nickel defense and rushing the linemen hard. However on a third and long they will often play six or seven defensive backs and try for the interception by double-covering all of the prime receivers.

When something the coach thinks will work doesn't, he needs to know why. How did the other team react that was different than expected, and how can this new reaction be attacked? He may have to keep in an extra blocker. Possibly the patterns will have to be run a few yards deeper or shorter in order to make them work.

A good coach must quickly find the strengths and weaknesses of the opponents, then attack them where they are weak. Darrell Royal, the former Texas coach, may have said it best when he said, "No use fartin' against thunder" and "Don't get in a pissin' contest with a skunk." Both ideas emphasize the obvious—that you don't want to go at your opponent's strengths.

Tactical Adjustments on Defense

Some teams will have several defensive teams ready depending on the tactical situation. There might be a regular defense, a nickel, a dime, a short-yardage (elephant), and a goal line defense. As a result, the offensive coordinator or the quarterback might wait until the defense is on the field before calling a play.

As a coach, if there is a 70 percent chance of a run you might substitute the short-yardage "elephant" defense. If there is a 70 percent chance of a pass you would probably put in the nickel or dime defense and rush the passer hard.

A few years ago, in the first game against New England, the Raiders threw deep seven times and completed one pass for 50 yards and another for a touchdown. When the two teams met again later that season in the playoff game, the Patriots wouldn't let the Raiders receivers deep. Doing so forced the Raiders to change their offensive strategy, which probably cost them the game.

Some coaches just count the number of wide receivers in the game to determine their defensive adjustment. Since a team can have from zero to five wide receivers in on any given play, it is often a good key indicating the type of play they have in mind—the more wide receivers, the better the chance that the play will be a pass.

Tactics in the Kicking Game

Sometimes nature, rather than the opposition, can be what forces a team to make tactical adjustments, especially with regard to the kicking game. A team might give up its option of receiving the kickoff in order to take the wind at its back. Or it may choose to go on defense because it has a strong defensive unit or because the field is wet or the stadium is windy. In the 1985 Rams versus Bears NFC championship game, John Robinson second-guessed himself after the game when he said that he should have taken the wind rather than kicked off when he had the chance. Former Rams coach and Bears assistant George Allen said after the game that when you play in Chicago you always take the wind if it is blowing more than 20 miles an hour.

From the Playbook

Fair catch: The opportunity for a receiving player to catch a kicked ball and not be tackled. It is signaled by waving one arm overhead. The ball cannot be advanced after making a fair catch.

Many people are not aware that in high school after a fair catch the receiving team has the option of taking a regular "scrimmage down" or a "free-kick down." A "scrimmage down" occurs automatically when a team takes a first and 10 option. A kickoff is an example of a free-kick down—where the opponents are not allowed to rush a kick. While it is not allowed to score three points if a kickoff sails over the goalposts, it is allowed on other free-kick downs. So if a team fair-catches a ball on its opponent's 30- or 40-yard line it has the option of sending in its kickoff team, and if the kicker kicks it through the uprights three points are scored. While this option is seldom used, it does win some games—for coaches who know the rules. A few years ago Vic Rowen, a past president of the American Football Coaches Association, was two points behind Cal Lutheran near the end of the game. Cal Lutheran punted short from its end zone. The San Francisco State safetyman fair-caught the punt. Vic sent in his kickoff team. They lined up in kickoff formation, and his placekicker split the uprights with his kick. Cal Lutheran was helpless to stop it because during a "free-kick" down the defense must remain at least 10 yards from the ball. Vic's knowledge of the rule allowed him to make a tactical decision that won the game by one point.

The more experienced coaches are more likely to be able to make the most effective tactical adjustments, thereby increasing the chances of winning. Wind, rain, fumbles and interceptions, penalties and emotional ups and downs, and unexpected scoring by either team are all factors that may require effective tactical decisions to increase the chances of victory. A pat on the back, a "chewing out," or running an offensive play or a defensive blitz that is "out of character" may have significantly positive effects on the outcome of the game.

Uprights: The vertical poles that extend up from the crossbar of the goalposts.

CHAPTER 12

Making the Big Plays and Converting Third Downs

Games are commonly won by the offensive team's success in converting a third down to a new first down. A series of successful conversions will probably result in a score. Big plays can also score, but they are difficult to plan and often require very specific defensive situations in which the offense can anticipate the defensive reactions. Field position, the score, the down, distance situation, and injuries to key defensive players can all help the offensive coordinator plan a big play.

Big Plays

Big plays can be planned for the offense or the defense. Some coaches believe that big play yards are more important than an equal number of yards gained in a drive. They can make the whole team more explosive and give it the confidence that it can score at any time.

The most successful coaches will watch hours of film looking for a number of ways to beat the upcoming opponent. One of the important concerns is where it will be possible to get a big offensive play. It might be a matchup, or it might be an adjustment to motion or a pattern that is giving this particular team trouble. It could be a defensive technique that might be exploited, especially with a defensive back. There are at least two openings in every alignment. Often there is an opening in the throwback area. Sometimes there is an opening in the wide countering (reverse) area. The openings are most likely to be in the area of the pass defense zones. Can the coach get a certain coverage with a formation or motion, then exploit it? Is there a simple read for the passer and receivers to look for that will break someone open?

Big Plays Must Be Denied by the Defense

Just as big plays by an offense can blow a game open, so too can the impact of a few big plays by the opposition. One team's big defensive plays can offset much of its opponent's advantage if the coach plans for them. What counts is not the opponent's ability to grind out the yardage but rather his ability to move the ball past the goal line. Whether it happens in a 15-play drive or a single big play, the results are the same.

Offset: A player lines up in a slightly different spot, such as a fullback lining up behind a guard or tackle, or a defensive lineman or linebacker lining up a half man or a man laterally, such as a nose tackle lining up on the side of the offensive center rather than being directly head up.

If the opponent has big play capability, who is most likely to be involved, and when is it most likely to happen? If in the past the team has looked for a big play when the defense was likely to be in a man-for-man coverage, it is essential that you know when your team is most likely to play man cover. Perhaps your opponent often looks for a big play from a screen pass when the defenders are most likely to blitz. If so, the defensive coach must either plan for blitzes in situations that are not common for him or he must make certain that the likely receivers in a screen pass are all covered by defenders. Who are you playing against? What plays or what players can cause you to lose? The coach must consider how his players can best match up against the opponent's best rusher and best receiver. He had better plan for them. He must plan to stop both the "who" and the "when"—the individual and the situation in which the player will be used.

Have you ever heard a coach do a postmortem on a game and say, "We really played well. If it hadn't been for those three big plays they made, it would have been our game"? Those three plays may have been a 50-yard pass, a 19-yard pass, and a 19-yard run in a tough situation. Three touchdowns or three critical first downs may have made the difference in the game. The defense didn't stop those big plays that won the game for their opponents.

Fielding a winning defense requires that you stop both big plays and long drives. While the other team's own penalties, missed assignments, or potential turnovers may stop a drive, a coach can't count on this outcome. He must be prepared to stop the drive by creating his own disruption, such as with a blitz.

How do the opponents try to get the big play? Do they try for a formation or a personnel mismatch? We would be less than astute if we played a rookie corner against Carolina's elite wide receiver, Steve Smith, for a whole game and let him take Steve one-on-one. The odds wouldn't favor our rookie!

How can a coach get extra help on the opposition's big playmaker? He might cover him man-to-man with the others playing zone. He might play one defender inside and another outside of him. What if the opponents are trying to get the ball to their best running back through screens and delays? A few years ago the Cowboys continually threw short to Emmitt Smith. Some teams let him catch it often under their zone coverage. Would you have put a spy on Emmitt to stop that 5-yard pass that he made 5 to 50 more yards on? The man-for-man "spy" could have eliminated a major part of that Cowboy offense.

Can you find a formation or down-and-distance tip-off? Are the opposing players more likely to pass when they must average at least five yards per play to get a first down? Are they more likely to pass from a split back set, where both running backs are set at least as wide as the offensive tackles? Will their big plays usually come on first down, from a particular set, with motion, or from outside their own 35? The more a coach knows, the better he can tip the odds in his favor. Then by discussing these tendencies with the players and practicing against the situations he can help to develop the *collective mentality* that will increase the odds for his team to win the situation.

Sometimes big plays can be predicted and stopped. "Their best receiver is not going to catch a quick post in the red zone this week against us. I don't care if we have to put three guys on him." The last several weeks, that play and that player have been *causing teams to lose*. Why would an intelligent team allow opponents to do what they like to do best? A coach should want them to have to try to beat his team "left-handed." He must make them try to beat his team with the things they don't like to do.

Third Downs

Third downs are similar to big plays in the effect they can have on a game's outcome. A positive or negative result for the offense on a third down can drastically change, or at least modify, what has happened in the previous downs in the drive. If as a coach you are in a critical drive and come up with a third and one, do you need a time-out to call a quarterback sneak? That would certainly be a waste of a time-out! Third down situations are always important for both the offense and the defense—they are impact areas that must be planned and practiced.

Both offensively and defensively, third down situations are like games unto themselves. They are the essential battles that can determine the outcome of the war. A team can continue a drive if it makes it on offense, and it can stop an opponent's drive if it wins the third down situation on defense. Winning the third down situations can override a lot of other factors. It's nice to make yards on first and second. It makes it easier to convert on third. But whatever the yardage, this is the pressure down. Offensively or defensively, teams only have to win one out of the three downs. They *must* win the third down war.

Frank Broyles, former Arkansas coach and athletic director, was the first to suggest that coaches only concern themselves with third down situations by having most of their scrimmages as third down scrimmages. Much later scripting came along. It made the third down situations being practiced much more exact—third and one on the 47 with the opponent's probable defense being an eagle, with tight man-for-man and the backers coming; or third and five with the probable defense a pro four-three and five-under two-deep coverage. Both the third down scrimmage and scripting helped us to coach situations, but they only took us a short way along the road to teaching the whole game. Third downs can be made more "game specific" by practicing in the red zone, goal line, and two-minute situations.

When You Must Throw

It is a good idea to have a pass play that will work against any cover: man, blitz, or zone. One such play is a shotgun, trips left, double slant in with the inside man slanting out. By having the "double slant in" it should work against a zone or a blitz. The inside receiver crossing the paths of the other two receivers should clear him if the defense is in man-to-man cover. If this is your "gotta have it" play it should be a part of the coach's seasonal theory of winning. It should underscore his week-to-week strategic plans.

The Blitz

The blitz is a dynamic member of the "impact family." Just as with a great actor, the blitz can play many roles and can change character often. The blitz can be a leading man, coming often during a game, or it can be a supporting player, coming onstage only occasionally. Mr. Blitz can be a stable character who is anticipated, or he can surprise us by coming when least expected. He can arrive quite normally, such as in a middle backer stunt, or be bizarre and exotic, like a safety or corner blitz. Whatever its guise, the blitz can have a dramatic impact on the outcome of a drive and of the game. Because of their importance, both the blitz and blitz pickup need to be practiced more than they will be used or seen in a game.

Some may say, "in this league we don't get blitzed a lot" or "we are really not a blitzing team" to explain why they don't need to work on their blitz on defense or blitz pickup on offense. Even so, coaches must practice on these for a significant amount of time or it will *cause them to lose* at some point.

Here's a hypothetical case: You are in the biggest game of the season. You need four points to win. You drive down the field. Third and five on the opponent's 24. You call a pass. Your passer drops, and here comes the blitz. You're sacked for a minus-seven. You didn't know how to pick up the blitz, and it caused you to lose. There are times when a team will need to blitz. There will be times when a team must pick up the blitz. These will happen in critical situations and, when done effectively, can *help a team to win*. Failing to pick up the blitz will ensure that it does not. An effective blitz can result in a big play for the defense. Effectively picking up the blitz can result in a big play for the offense.

Planning a Blitz

How a team will blitz is a major concern. Coaches evaluate what blitzes have been successful against an opponent in the past. If the team has had trouble with a strong-side two-backer blitz two weeks in a row, shouldn't they try it? A coach should know the plan of his team's opponents in reaction to a blitz. Do they use a hot receiver? Do they hold in their backs, or might they quick-release a back in a "hot" pattern? If the tight end or the slot back is the likely "hot" receiver, the coach might disguise a man coverage or shorten the zones to stop it. If the opponents hold their backs in to block, the defensive rushers might concentrate their rush on one side where they can outnumber the blockers. Or the coach might decide to commit more players to the defensive secondary and look for an interception. If it is a blitz situation, will they go to maximum protection and throw? If so, what patterns are likely? Will they throw slants, or is a run a possibility?

Coaches check their scouting reports for the likely runs—a quick pitch, a sweep, or a draw trap. Be prepared for what the opponents are likely to do. Can their quarterback scramble, and if so which is his most likely direction? How will the non–drop back actions (waggle, boot, sprint out, roll out, rove) be handled? A coach should assign players to contain that expected movement so that the blitz can be successful.

Scramble: The running of the quarterback after he has been forced out of the pocket on a pass play.

Blitz Pickup

A few years ago a major motel chain promoted its inns with the slogan "No bad surprises." This slogan is also appropriate in building an offensive unit's alertness to being blitzed. Nothing can blow apart an offensive play as quickly as an effective blitz. "Bad surprises" range from a loss, to an interception or fumble lost, to the loss of a ballcarrier or quarterback due to a blindside hit. Any of these bad surprises can cause a team to lose, so the offense must be prepared to neutralize any blitz.

The entire offensive unit, both staff and players, must be on a constant "red alert" for a blitz. At any level of football the quarterback should be taught about and drilled to be prepared for the blitz and know what to do against it until the "all clear" has sounded. He should be aware of any signals the defense gives to indicate a possible blitz—tight bump cover, linebackers or safeties who have moved up, or an important substitution may signal the heightened possibility for a blitz. Just one player asleep at the wheel can cause a disaster. This is another area in which the coach must develop that *collective mentality* that puts everybody on the same page.

When an offense has developed a high level of confidence in its ability to pick up and exploit the blitz, it often plays with a confident attitude that seems to say, "Bring it on, baby."

CHAPTER 13

Scoring in the Scoring Zones

◆◆◆◆◆◆◆◆◆◆◆◆◆◆◆◆◆◆◆◆◆◆◆◆◆◆◆◆◆◆◆◆

The most effective coaches practice scoring every day. It is the movement of the ball, particularly in the scoring zones, that generally determines who will win. Because of this, red zone attack and defense are extremely interesting to plan for and to practice. This is where the coaches must concentrate their efforts and the players must play with intelligence, intensity, and impact.

A team can complete three or four 15-yard curls or drive the ball 60 yards, but unless its efforts show up on the scoreboard it is just exercise. It's nice to be able to amass 200 yards of running offense or complete 60 percent of passes, but the records that last are in the win-loss column. Will the record be 10–0 or 0–10? Practicing scoring will increase your wins.

Some very effective teams do most of their practice from the 30 or 40 on in. Heck, if the play is good in the fringe area, it is probably good inside your 20 or between the 30s. It is easier to assume the efficiency of an effective red zone play working from your own 30 than it is to assume that a play that works near your 30 will work in the red zone.

Jousting between the 20s doesn't win the game. What wins the game is generally what your team does from the opponent's 20 or 30 on in and what the other team can do from your 20 in. That's crunch time!

On the other side of the ball, the starting defenders are getting the picture of the kinds of tactics other teams employ on the goal line. Maybe they can get two extra stops per season by being experienced in goal line defense. Instead of having a 5–5 record, the team is now 7–3. The games may have been even.

The team may not joust any better than its opponents. But they won because of their strong goal line play—goal line offense or goal line defense.

Two analogies from other sports can point to the importance of actually scoring touchdowns, not just running plays. In golf the object is to get the ball in the hole in as few strokes as possible. Top teaching pros emphasize that the best way for the high-handicap golfer to lower his or her score is not to go to the driving range and slam away for distance, but rather to spend about 70 percent of his or her time practicing the shots that will score from 100 yards in. The approach shots, the pitches and chips, and the putts are the shots that actually put the ball in the hole—thus lowering your score. In basketball, imagine how ridiculous it would be for a team to spend two hours running fast breaks and set plays but never attempting a shot. The team might get lots of players open, but it wouldn't convert to points on the board.

The "Gotta Score" Area

Fringe area (outside the 30-yard line): Take a shot—the defense is not yet compressed.

Red zone area (from 25 yards in): Reduction of field depth reduces the area for the defensive team to defend.

Goal area, 20–15 yards: Where does the opponent change his style of defense?

15–10 yards: You want to be your best here, so practice it.

Goal line: Where does the opponent's real goal line defense begin?

Win with reps—not tricks!

Once your team is in the "gotta score" area, all three scoring zones (red zone, goal area, and goal line) provide the opportunity to execute point-scoring plays. Coaches want to develop a scoring plan with specific concepts and plays for each zone. Coaches who work hard on their red zone game, both offense and defense, will not only develop their team's competency in play execution but will also develop a greater motivation in their players; because of their confidence, the team will play more intensely. Confidence in execution is definitely preferable to creativity.

Confidence should enable your team to play more effectively. The other impact areas we have discussed become even more important as your team advances toward the goal line or is backed up deep in its own territory. The importance of avoiding the penalty, causing a fumble, thwarting a blitz, and converting on third or fourth down are all magnified here in the scoring zone. Attention to these *impact* details in every practice and in the other areas of the field makes your goal line offense or defense more productive. It is like having several streams flowing together to make a rushing river—attention to these impact areas will combine to make a team far more effective where it counts the most.

Red Zone Offense

The play in the red zone is the most competitive area of what is probably the most competitive game in the world. Scoring points here, or denying them, is what the game is all about. How do you see the teams you are watching attacking or defending the goal line? The chances are that the defense will be more predictable from the 20 on. How would you attack the defense here? Can you notice any tendencies? Would you blitz here? When? Is the defense playing man-to-man?

Field space dictates the offense because of how the defense uses the field. If the ball is on the 50, the defense has 60 yards of field depth to defend (through the back of the end zone). By the time the ball reaches the 15, there is only a 25-yard depth to defend. The defense may commit more people to stop the run or rush the passer. Man-to-man defense has a better chance to work because there is less area for the receiver to find an opening in. The offense may have run out of space to throw certain patterns, and the defense will change to reflect that advantage. So as the defense changes, the offense will have to look to see where the advantages are. Is it in a man-to-man matchup where the offense may be able to shake a receiver free? Will a crossing pattern or boot action work? Can the team run the option? Will a quick trap work? Many teams will increase their blitzing in their red zone defense. On the other hand, some teams never seem to blitz. You certainly shouldn't see any three-deep formations—if the defensive players have any brains at all—because there are no deep zones to defend, only the short and intermediate areas.

Goal Line Offense

Coaches must answer these questions in order to be able to attack the defense effectively as the ball nears the goal line. When does a team go into its true goal line defense? If the defenders are man-to-man, how do they contain the quarterback? Is the bootleg pass or run open? Will crossing patterns work? Can they get outside? How about a run-pass option? If the true goal line defense is a hard-charging six- or eight-man line, a trap might work. Once man-to-man pass defense is expected, a crossing pattern that may screen off a defender might be used. If the team doesn't contain the quarterback effectively and attacks the running back, a bootleg play with the quarterback faking to a back and then running wide in the opposite direction often works. How powerful is your team? The more potential power it has, the more it can reduce its formations and get into a jousting contest. If your team is not a big physical team, or if your opponents are more physical than you are, the coach could use a spread, forcing the defense to spread out. The coach should also figure out how he might get his best people against the opponent's weakest people. There might be possibilities of getting a mismatch through motion, possibly by putting a wide receiver into a set back position where he is likely to be covered by a slower backer, then motion him out and free him up for the touchdown with crosses or picks.

As a coach you would run the stuff that works on the goal line. Putting in a special play for this week's goal line attack may not be as wise as running your basic stuff, or running your basic stuff with a wrinkle, such as from a different set or with motion. Could you take away their best middle backer by motioning your fullback? If so, you wouldn't have to worry about blocking him. Coaches should pick their "tried and true" plays based on personnel or formation matchups.

The game really changes down in the red zone. Does your team try to power the ball over, or does it try to sneak a receiver out? There are so many important factors in this part of the game to observe and analyze.

CHAPTER 14

Penalties and Turnovers—the Viruses That Can Kill You

◆◆◆◆◆◆◆◆◆◆◆◆◆◆◆◆◆◆◆◆◆◆◆◆◆◆◆◆◆◆◆◆

A virus enters your body and makes you sick, sometimes terminally. Another kind of virus can enter your computer and cause it to malfunction or become inoperable. Similarly the habit of committing fouls that cause you to be penalized can infect a team like a virus and cause it to be ineffective, or worse, cause it to lose.

Penalties

The various fouls may carry a 5-, 10-, or 15-yard penalty, possibly an automatic first down, and rarely, a score can be awarded. For most penalties, if the offense has run a play and there was an offensive or defensive penalty, the offended team has the option to allow the play to stand or to disregard it, go back to the original down and distance, and then have the penalty assessed. So if the offense gained 15 yards and there was a 5-yard penalty against the defense, the offense would refuse the penalty. Or if the defense stopped the play for a loss or no gain but the offense was guilty of a five-yard penalty, the defense might well refuse the penalty. In penalties assessed against a team near its own end zone, the penalty is assessed at half the distance to the goal line rather than the 5, 10, or 15 yards called for otherwise. There are about a hundred different penalties.

Common Penalties

Encroachment or offside occurs when a defensive player encroaches into the neutral zone, the line of scrimmage, before the ball is snapped. It is a five-yard penalty.

Illegal procedure can indicate any number of minor offenses such as an illegal formation, the back in motion running forward, or an illegal shift.

Holding carries a 5-yard penalty if against the defense and a 10-yard penalty if against the offense.

Pass interference occurs when an offensive receiver or a defensive back interferes with the opportunity of his opponent to make a catch when that player has a clear chance to do so. At the pro level the ball is spotted where the interference occurred. For high school and college it is a 15-yard penalty and an automatic first down.

Illegal blocks include clipping (blocking in the back) and blocking below the waist. Both of these are illegal except within a few yards of the offensive center immediately after the ball has been snapped. A chop block, also illegal, occurs during a double-team block when the defender is stood up by one player while a teammate drives into the defender's knee, risking severe injury.

Personal fouls include actions deemed by the officials to be unnecessary roughness. They carry a 15-yard penalty and the possibility of being ejected from the game. Hitting the passer or kicker after their action is completed or hitting a ballcarrier after he is downed or out-of-bounds are examples.

Unsportsmanlike conduct is a non-contact foul by a player or coach, and sometimes a spectator. It includes verbal abuse and activities that may demean the other team or an official. An excessive celebration after a touchdown, especially one that calls attention to the scorer, is another example. This is a 15-yard penalty.

Helmet-related penalties include touching or grabbing an opponent's face mask. This might cause a severe neck twist. Also, no players can use the top of the helmet as a weapon. The head must be up in all contact in order to protect the neck from injury, especially a compression type of injury.

Delay of game penalties are five-yard penalties that are imposed when either team is not ready to play after the referee has signaled the ball is ready for play.

Bobby Bowden, of Florida State, says that penalties are coaching mistakes. You can eliminate many penalties with effective coaching. Avoiding penalties is a very important part of the mental game of football. During the writing of this chapter a highly ranked team was called for 14 penalties one week and had 8 in the first quarter of its next game, costing it two scores. About five penalties per game is average for a good team.

Can you imagine any coach signing a contract to play a game where the terms of the contract mandate that he has to start six of his possessions with a first and 15 or a first and 25? That would give his team too great a disadvantage at the start of the game. But any coach who allows his team to commit fouls that lead to penalties is basically doing the same thing. He is allowing his players to put the team in a significant execution disadvantage where they have to be clearly superior to the other team just to get back to being even.

Every coach wants to avoid penalties. But how much do they work on it? North Carolina basketball teams under Dean Smith always got fewer fouls than their opponents. Fans of the visiting team would chant, "Carolina refs, Carolina refs," thinking Carolina was getting a break, when the fact was that the players were coached against fouling. For example, they would never try to block a perimeter jump shot. When you try to block an outside shot in basketball, you will probably be carried into the shooter, who is probably moving somewhat forward. So the NC players were taught only to jump straight up, hoping to bother the shooter, perhaps making him increase the arc of his shot. After all, the jump shot is a rather low-percentage shot, so why give the shooter two free throws by fouling?

Certainly fouls impact a football game just as they do a basketball game. If a basketball team gives up 15 more fouls than the other team, that fouling team will have to be a great deal better in all the other areas to win the game. It is the same in football. A 5-yard penalty on first down makes it first and 5 or first and 15—depending on which team committed the foul. If you are on offense, you now have either three downs to make 5 yards (1.7 yards a play) or three downs to make 15 yards (5 yards a play). It doesn't take a genius to figure out which situation is preferred on either side of the ball.

I remember a junior college game in Los Angeles between two fierce rivals. Valley College was the stronger team but lost because its middle backer was called for nine 15-yard roughness penalties. Physically the player had great potential. But did his presence in the game make his team 135 yards better than if his sub had been in there? He single-handedly lost the game by repeat-edly giving Pierce College first downs, which led directly to their win.

Historically Speaking Some years ago Penn State was playing Kansas. With 30 seconds left, Penn State scored, making it 13–14. They went for two and failed—but the yellow flag signaled a problem. Kansas had 12 men on the field. After a yard and a half penalty, Penn State went for two again and made it, winning 15–14. Not all penalties so dramatically affect the outcome of the game in the final seconds, but any penalty at any time during the game can have an effect that loses the game for one of the teams. It could be a five-yard motion penalty on third down on the 40. But that one little insignificant penalty might have stopped a drive that could otherwise have scored.

The situation in which the penalty occurs can make the penalty even more critical. A player being offside when another player blocks a kick or some-one behind the kick returner clipping an opponent and thereby nullifying a long gain or a touchdown are common examples. Some years ago when Paul Dietzel won the national championship at LSU, every snap of the year was on "one." His thinking was that he didn't want his team jumping offside by chang-ing snap counts. It just gave them one more thing to think about. A holding penalty against the offense in the red zone may not only be a 10-yard penalty, it may be a four-point penalty if the team can't make the touchdown and must kick a field goal. Similarly, an offensive penalty in the two-minute situation can cause a team to lose the impetus of its drive and seriously reduce its chance to score. On the other hand, a defensive penalty in the two-minute situation can increase the offensive team's impetus and lead to a game-winning score.

In a game of football, the ball moves up and down the field. It doesn't mat-ter whether a player carries it or the referee carries it—the yards all count the same. So you can see why you might win the jousting contest in terms of your offense beating the other team's defense, but you can still lose the game by not taking care of the business of winning. Heck, if you've got the ball and you are moving backward toward the goal you are trying to defend, something is wrong with your team—and the coach's teaching.

What kind of a mind-set does the coach form for his team? Does he want to avoid penalties, or does he want to have to overcome the dumb mistakes his team makes time after time? For a coach, it's just like raising children. If you put up with a messy room, you get a messy room. If you put up with loud music, you get loud music. If you put up with penalties, you will get penalties. Whatever you tolerate, you'll get. If you tolerate a top player getting two pass interference penalties a game, you'll get it. "Coach I was just trying to make a play!" It doesn't matter. If the foul is called at the spot, as it is in the pros, and you have two 35-yard interference penalties, that's 70 yards you just added to the opponent's offense.

Turnovers

Turnovers can happen with a bad center snap, a poor handoff, inefficient ball-carrying technique, a hard tackle, a stripping of the ball from the ballcarrier during the run or during the tackle, an interception, a fumble recovery, or a blocked kick. Coaches need to prevent their own team's turnovers and increase their opponents' turnovers.

Effective coaches use drills to prevent turnovers by their team and to increase the turnovers by the other team. Learning to carry the ball is an important technique. The hand should be cupped over the end of the ball, there should be pressure along the forearm and elbow, and the ball should be held firmly against the body with the hand higher than the elbow. Another skill to be taught is to cover the ball with both hands when being tackled or falling. When falling, it is natural to put out an arm to break the fall. This increases the chance of dislocating a shoulder or breaking a collarbone on the extended arm. It also increases the chance of fumbling.

 What to Watch For   Notice in games how often pro and college running backs carry the ball away from the body—and fumble.

Passers should be taught to throw short passes low. A high short pass can be deflected upward and then intercepted by the converging defensive backs. Quarterbacks should also be taught to keep their elbows close to the body when dropping to pass. It is more natural to hold the ball with the elbows wide, but this allows a blindside pass rusher to drive his arms inside the elbow, rip downward, and strip the passer of the ball.

Defensive players are often taught several ways to strip the runner of the ball. If the tackler is coming up from behind the runner and the ball is being carried low, he can grab the front of the ball and rip it downward. If the ballcarrier is not holding the ball tight to his body the tackler can punch it forward, driving his fist between the ballcarrier's elbow and body. If the defender is approaching from the front and the ballcarrier is already being tacked by a teammate, the second defender to arrive can lift the ballcarrier's elbow with one hand and punch the ball back with the other.

The Stats Tell the Story

The statistics don't lie, but we have to look at *all* of the stats to get the complete picture of a game's outcome. Generally the team that gets the most total yards wins. All of the yards count the same—yards gained by running, yards gained by passing, yards gained by punting, and yards gained by the referee walking off penalties.

Here is a fictional, but common, example of game statistics. How do you read them?

	Wildcats	Cougars
Net yards rushing	200	100
Passes attempted	20	10
Passes completed	10	5
Net yards passing	125	50
Total yards	325	150

Who won the game? Probably the Wildcats by three to seven points because they had a 175-yard edge on yardage. But no! The Cougars won by two touchdowns. Those stats don't show the hidden yardage.

You can generally figure that every lost fumble costs you 40 or more yards. (You didn't get the punt yardage, and you had no opportunity to gain more first downs.) Each interception of a short pass is worth 30 to 40 yards. Long passes intercepted are not as harmful, especially if they are 40 yards or more—then they are the same as a punt. A blocked kick should be worth at least 50 yards, and with work it can be turned into much more yardage and often a touchdown.

	Wildcats	Cougars
Passes had intercepted	2 (−70)	0
Number of punts	3	6
Yardage on punts	+90	+180
Return yardage	+20	+30
Fumbles lost	3 (−120)	0
Punts had blocked	1 (−60)	0
Number of penalties	9 (−95)	5 (−35)
Hidden (non-offense) yards	110 − 345 = −235	210 − 35 = 175

So the 150 yards that the offensive stats show for the Cougars was actually closer to 325 yards in total (150 offensive yards plus 175 "hidden" yards). But the Wildcats' 325 offensive yards are actually reduced by 235 yards for a net of 90 yards.

Coaches who are focused on overall team performance know this, so they are more likely to work on ball stripping on defense and ball protection on offense. They are more likely to work on fumble recovery techniques. They are more likely to work on effective punt blocking techniques along with correct loose ball pickup skills for the non-blocking rushers. They are more likely to work on execution in the kicking game and forcing their opponents into mistakes.

Now let's look at these factors in two real games. A few years ago the first two games of Wake Forest went this way. The opening game was against Appalachian State. Wake Forest was ready to execute—it had 22 first downs and State had 12. Wake Forest ran 87 plays for 502 yards in 36 minutes, and their opponents ran 51 plays for 247 yards in 23 minutes. Wake Forest won the joust. But the scoreboard at the end of the game showed that Wake Forest lost 25 to 27. How could they possibly have lost?

And now, as Paul Harvey would say, "for the rest of the story." Wake had six penalties for 42 yards, State had two for 15. Wake had five giveaways, State had none. A lot of the offensive production never got to the scoring zone because of turnovers. Wake had no big plays in the game. State had one long touchdown pass. On punts Appalachian had 126 more net yards. Appalachian was two for two on field goals. Wake Forest missed its only attempt. In the scoring zone, because of takeaways and a missed field goal, Wake Forest got only two touchdowns in three trips to the red zone. Appalachian had one drive to the red zone and scored on it. State scored on two of Wake Forest's turnovers.

Historically Speaking		Wake Forest	Appalachian State
	First downs	22	12
	Plays	87 (502 yards)	51 (247 yards)
	Time of possession	36:51	23:09
	Penalties/yards	6 (42 yards)	2 (15 yards)
	Fumbles lost	5	0
	Big plays	0	1
	Punts/average yards	3 (49 yards)	7 (39 yards)
	Total yards punting	147	273
	Returns	0	0
	Field goals (points/attempts)	0/1	2/2
	In scoring zone	3 times for 14 points	1 time for 7 points
	% of possible points scored	67%	100%
	Total score	25	27

A couple of years earlier Wake Forest had recruited two great runners. They were largely responsible for the 500-plus yards of offense in that game. They were also responsible for the five fumbles. The next week they were put on the bench and a slow non-fumbling back played. In that game Wake Forest had 13 first downs and Virginia Tech had 22. Tech had 437 yards to Wake's 175. Tech had the ball for 11 more minutes than Wake Forest, but Tech lost its only game of the season, 13–6. How did that happen? Wake had 4 penalties for 30 yards; Tech had 14 for 163 yards. So the referee carried the ball a lot for Wake Forest that day. Tech had three giveaways, Wake had one. Wake had one big play, Tech had none. Wake picked up 141 yards more in punting. Wake had 57 more yards on kick returns. Wake got in the scoring zone once and scored. Tech was in the scoring zone six times and kicked two field goals. They had the potential of scoring 42 points but only got 6.

	Wake Forest	Virginia Tech
Historically Speaking First downs	13	22
Plays	58 (175 yards)	79 (437 yards)
Time of possession	24:33	35:27
Penalties/yards	4 (30 yards)	14 (163 yards)
Fumbles lost	1	3
Big plays	1	0
Punts/average yards	7 (51 yards)	6 (36 yards)
Total yards punting	357 yards	216 yards
Returns	1 (75 yards)	1 (18 yards)
Field goals	0/0	2/3
In scoring zone	1 time for 7 points	6 times for 6 points
% of possible points scored	100%	28%
Score	13	6

When you add Wake Forest's 175 yards from plays, 357 from punts, and 75 from the punt return, then subtract the 30 yards of penalties, you get a total yardage of 577 for Wake Forest. Then add Virginia Tech's 437 total offense yards, 216 on punts, and 18 on the punt return and subtract its 163 penalty yards, and Tech has a total of 508 yards. That is fairly even. Then factor in the plus-two ratio on turnovers and you get about another 80 yards for Wake Forest. That brings its approximate yardage to 657. That is almost a 150-yard difference in yardage between the two teams. Then consider the one big play for Wake Forest and the red zone efficiency in scoring, and you have the game.

Despite the misperceptions of fans, commentators, players, and coaches, the team that played the best game of football won both of the games we just cited. Just how good was the team that had 14 penalties and three turnovers, missed an easy field goal, and blew a coverage that resulted in a score? Just how good is a team that gets into the scoring zone six times and because of penalties and turnovers gets only six points? Is that team really worth much on that day? Obviously the game is not just about how many yards a team makes on offense. The *game* is far more than that.

CHAPTER 15
Handling the Clock

For the spectator, as for the coach, the clock should be a consideration for more than the two-minute warning. Clock concerns could start with several minutes to go. The clock is a factor whether a team is ahead or behind. Many people think of "beating the clock" only when a team is driving with 30 seconds left. Often the game is already decided by that time, and only a miracle could change the outcome—like the rare two scores in the last two minutes that LSU did against Alabama recently or the three touchdowns in the last two minutes that Weber State produced some years ago.

 Two-minute offense or two-minute drill: The attack used by a team late in a half when it is behind and attempting to score while conserving time.

In handling the clock a team must have at its disposal both the plays and the *collective mentality* of how to use them. It needs plays to bleed the clock (inbounds runs, safe passes) and plays to stop the clock (out-of-bounds or high-percentage first down plays that require the clock to be stopped as the chains are moved).

When good teams practice, it is common to set situations such as the following:

- You are six points down, you have one time-out, and the defense has three. You are on your own 35.

- You are two points down with the ball on your 20. Your field goal kicker is accurate from the 25. You have three minutes and two time-outs.

A difference of one point or one time-out can significantly alter how a coach will play those last few minutes or seconds. And while he may sometimes be in that "must win" situation with 30 seconds left, and without Joe Montana or John Elway directing his forces, the coach will often find himself at the end of the first half with the game very much in doubt. As a coach you need a plan for how you will score and how you will use your time-outs.

End of the Half

Very often at the end of the half, situations can occur that can dramatically affect the outcome of the game. Let's say we're in a big game. We are the underdog, but we are ahead 10–3, and we get the ball with 1:10 left on our own 30. We know we will get the ball on the next half kickoff, so we have back-to-back possessions. What if we get into our two-minute offense, throw three incompletions, and the other team gets the ball back and scores—now it's 10–10. Our mishandling of the clock may have just cost us the game. Really, the most important thing for players and coaches in this situation is to go into the second half at 10–3. We don't have to score to be ahead, and if we screw up we are tied after working our hearts out for 30 minutes.

Or let's say we're on defense. We've fought like hell. It's the last minute of the half, and the opposing team just kicked a field goal and it is 10–7. How we finish the half will have an effect on how the third quarter will be played. Can we get a field goal and go into the locker room tied? Maybe with effective planning and playing we might even get a touchdown. That would certainly affect the psychological momentum!

Why do football teams have to practice two-minute situations? Because they occur every week and they can deeply impact the game. The coach needs a theory of how to handle each situation, ahead or behind. Who receives the next kickoff? Which team is more fired up? Let's say we are the underdog and we're tied at 7. We have the ball with three time-outs. We have 1:23 left in the half. We should have our "collective mentality" working here. We might spread them out with three wideouts and run. We might throw short high-percentage passes. We want to keep the ball in-bounds. We have worked on the importance of not having penalties during this phase of the game. If I'm coaching, I really just want to get off at 7–7. We run the draw and get six yards. We run a screen and get six more. We're not trying to score. We throw a slant, and our receiver breaks a tackle and runs to their 42. Now the whole scenario has changed. We have now added 50 yards to our total stats, but these yards are useless unless we score. Because *points win*! Now I can try to aggressively move the ball into field goal range, kick it, and end the half up by three points. Even if we miss the field goal there will probably be too little time for the opponents to do much with it. My team has to realize how the two-minute situation can change in mid-drive. We must have practiced it.

Let's say that our field goal kicker's range is from the 23 in. So we have three plays and three time-outs to make 19 yards. Now we have to be aggressive with the ball. It's not enough now to go for the short-yardage plays. But we must not throw an interception. The team is aware of all this because we have practiced it—maybe not this week, but within the last three. And we have practiced it in the spring and frequently during the season.

Add a 21-yard pass to the equation, and now the ball is on the 21. We have the option of falling down three times and kicking. But we still have our time-outs, and now we may even have a chance for a touchdown. The scenario has changed again! So we need to protect our field goal possibility, but if we can get a touchdown we are just that much better off.

So the coaches and team have switched thoughts:

- From "Let's just punt to them with as few seconds as possible on the clock" to

- "Let's get the field goal" to

- "Let's protect the field goal but go for the touchdown."

We will therefore take an aggressive shot at scoring while still protecting one time-out to allow us to get our field goal team in easily. So while the quarterback sees three time-outs up on the scoreboard, he has to realize that he can only use two.

With three time-outs per half, most coaches would like to save them for tactical purposes at the end of the half when they might be needed to slow the usage of the clock by the opponents if they are ahead. But sometimes the time-outs must be used for injuries or for critical situations in which the opponents surprise with a different offensive or defensive formation.

End of the Game

You know, whether on offense or defense, that at the end of the game when the offensive team is behind by seven or fewer points it must get into scoring position—and it must score! It must be practiced, or everyone will be left with an adrenaline rush but no points. As an offensive coach you call your first play and have your second in mind—but if that first play breaks for big yardage, the situation has changed, so you must adapt to it with your next play.

As a defensive coach, say the other team has 80 yards to go in two minutes. You want to force your opponents into having to hit eight straight passes in order to beat you. So you play some zone, some man-to-man with a free safety, and play the waiting game. But a draw play may hit for 60 yards. Now your thinking must be much more aggressive. A blitz may be a great choice. The offensive team is in a "hurry up" mode. The players race out to the ball, they're excited about scoring— but they may have forgotten about picking up a possible blitz.

It reminds me of a time I was listening to a local team's first game of the season. The team was favored at home and behind by three in the last two minutes. The announcer assured the radio fans that there was nothing to worry about because the team practiced its two-minute offense every Friday. From my point of view, they had a lot to worry about. They had probably practiced running off tackle every practice that week, yet they found only 10 minutes the day before the game to practice the situation that would bring either smiles or tears. The outcome was not surprising. The home team turned the ball over on the fourth down without crossing the 50. Suffering an upset on that opening day threw the team into a tailspin that ruined a promising season.

If you were playing golf you would have putts that are straight, putts that break from right to left, putts that break from left to right. You'd have three-inch putts and 70-foot putts and everything in between. The same is true in the "beat the clock" situations. Even if you had the ball on the 25-yard line 20 times it would never be the same. One time you are ahead, another time you are behind. One time it's a blitzing team, another time it's a zone team. One time you have no time-outs left, the next time you have three time-outs. One time you hit the first play and the ball is on the five, another time you get sacked on the first play.

As a high school coach, you might plan to never deviate from your core offense. You might not approach it like the pros or the big universities. Rather than send out four wide receivers, you might stay in your basic pro I set the whole time. But you have to have a plan, and you have to practice it. And you must practice enough of the varying situations that your team is comfortable with changing situations.

We talk about the two-minute situation often. It is really an intriguing part of the game—and at the pro level the team had better have it down pat. Certainly at the high school level players need to do a great deal of thinking and practicing on the offensive and defensive situations. The team needs to be confident during those last two minutes when the game is on the line. It certainly warrants more time than most coaches give it—at any level.

Certainly before the defense goes into the game in the two-minute situation we want to remind the players of the situation. Suppose your offense is in the game and you are ahead by one with a minute to go in the game. The coach might tell his defense, "They have used all of their time-outs, so even if we have to punt, they won't have the luxury of calling a time-out. They will have to go to the sidelines, and as a result we will want to be in a cover six or seven. They like the screen, so who is the spy? Just play the way we practiced, and remember—no penalties." So the coach can briefly remind his team of what they have already discussed in team meetings, reminding the team that the offense will want to run or pass to the sidelines so they can stop the clock and conserve time. He can also remind them of the pass defenses and the covers that should work against the offense's probable plays. It is also important to stay calm and just talk the team through the defenses for the expected attack. The coach might also want to remind them of the opponent's favorite drive starters and of the defense practiced for the expected situation.

Considerations When the Team Must Score

If the regular offense hasn't been winning, the coach may need another offense—an offense that will allow him to get his best scoring people on the field with plays that can win. While the running offense or a balanced attack may work through most of the game, an attack that highlights passing is necessary when the team must win in the last few moments of the game. During most of the game the coach may have taken the position that "When you pass four things can happen—and three of them are bad." But now the team must score, so he will have to go against the normal odds and look to the pass and the pass-related plays (draws and screens) to win the game.

A coach should limit the formations and plays. A few teams have limited their two-minute offense to one play, five yard outs, with the receivers breaking to the sidelines after a five-yard release. Others keep their whole offense available in their two-minute package. One approach is too simple, the other too complex. A coach might limit his offense to one or two formations, with the possibility of adding another set for a given opponent. The basic "run and shoot" set, with two split ends and two inside slot backs, works well. With four immediate eligible receivers the defense can be attacked more effectively. Then by sending a slot back in motion to the other side a new problem is caused for the defense. The quarterback can be under the center or in a shotgun set.

Will three points win it, or will it take seven or eight? This will determine the number of yards the team must cover in the number of seconds remaining. How many seconds to move how many yards? This limitation can certainly reduce the types of plays the coach will call. If there's a minute and a half to go 80 yards, there will be about 11 seconds to go each 10 yards. What kinds of plays will make this happen? The real question is what kinds of plays will be able to stop the clock because a player has run out of bounds or because the ball has moved at least 10 yards and the chains must be reset (at the pro level the latter is only a factor when a measurement is called for). The defense is not about to give an easy post pattern, and the offense will only have about 5 to 12 seconds per play. With this much time the quarterback can throw passes that are more likely to be completed.

In designing a two-minute offense, coaches will want patterns that will be effective against both two- and three-deep coverages with both man or zone in the underneath areas. Then when the blitz comes, which it should if you have been successful, the patterns must also work against man-to-man cover. (Properly taught, hooks and curls work well.) Additionally, if the team gets into the red zone it will need to have plays that have good chances of crossing the goal line.

But the team also needs clock-stopping possibilities. While the coach would like to save the last time-out for a possible last play attempt at a touchdown or field goal, he may want to give priority to the possibility of his quarterback being sacked. This is a good time to use your last time-out because the play will eat up far too many seconds while the players unravel, the play is called, and the formation is set.

If you were the coach, what would your last play of the game be if you had to have a touchdown? You might consider having three plays—a play that would work from the 15 in, one from the 35 to the 15, and one that can score from farther out. The latter two could both be the jump ball (Hail Mary, Big Ben) type of pass with several receivers going into the same area, with one or two behind and one ahead of the primary receiver(s) and ready to play the tipped and batted passes.

Primary receiver: The first choice of the passer in a pass pattern.

If you only need a field goal, your scoring zone area changes. Instead of having to get to the goal line, you will only need to consider getting to the 25 (or whatever yard line is within your kicker's range). So you need a play that will get you to that field goal range area. Since each kicker is different and wind and weather can change the area from which he will be accurate, the coach must keep these options in mind when planning the season's two-minute theory and making tactical decisions during the game.

Pass Patterns vs. Common Defenses During the Last Two Minutes

If the defense plays man-to-man to stop short passes, use

- Crossing patterns
- Clear with three deep routes and drag one man
- Clear two deep (to eliminate underneath "man" cover people) and cross two

If the defense plays zone under (five or six zones), use

- Curl-flat combination (reading widest underneath zone)
- Quick screen

If the defense uses two deep safeties, use

- Four verticals (four deep routes)

If the defense uses three deep safeties, use

- Passes that attack the weak side

For running plays against man-to-man defense, use

- Quarterback draw
- Boot

For running plays against zone defense, use

- Power plays

Playing for the Last-Second Field Goal

With no time-outs left you might get the ball to the middle of the field on one play, then stop the clock on the next to allow your field goal team to get into the game.

Winning the *game* requires a great deal of thinking, planning, and teaching so that the team has every tool necessary to avoid losing and increase its chances of victory—a sound offense that fits the players, effective defensive potentials that the players can utilize, along with the planning and teaching for making effective tactical adjustments, avoiding turnovers and penalties, and all the other concerns of the game that the coaches must plan for and teach. And there is never enough time to do it all.

PART IV

Enjoying the Games of Football

CHAPTER 16

How to Watch a Game

There are lots of ways to watch a football game. Your son is playing his first high school game. Your eyes will be glued on him. Maybe you are watching your alma mater play its homecoming game. You might just watch the ball and see the runs, the passes, and the big hits—just sit close to the 50-yard line and settle back with a hot dog and a Coke. If you prefer the comfort and catering of home, you can enjoy your 50-yard-line seat as well as the parade of instant replays that dissect every pass, catch, and tackle. But what if you want to understand the intricacies of the game and see it as a coach might?

Where to Sit at a Game

Sitting on the 50, you can see how many yards each play gained or lost. But if you sit in the end zone, preferably with binoculars, you can see the details better. You may not see immediately how much yardage is gained, but you can see the spacing between the linemen. The pulling of the guards or other linemen and the crossing of defenders in stunts and blitzes is more visible. It is easy to see the inside or outside shades of the defensive backs and how they drop into their zones or how they handle the receiver's moves in a man-on-man defense. You can observe the spacing of the backs and whether or not a back cheats out or in on certain plays. So you can sit in the end zone, as coaches prefer, and see the width of the game, or sit on the 50 and absorb the depth of the game. Also you will want to sit fairly high. The lower you are the worse your view of the game. Coaches on the field have the worst view in the house!

We remember being invited to a Pac 10 game at the Rose Bowl when Terry Donahue was coaching there. The first eight rows are used only when there is a sellout crowd, so Terry's seats were in the ninth row, and right on the 50. If you wanted to see the backs of the UCLA uniforms but not see the field through the blue and gold human wall, they were great seats. Our wives were happy, but we wanted to see the game, so we moved to the general admission seats behind the end zone, about halfway up, and enjoyed an interesting afternoon of football.

What to Focus On

Now, assuming you want to see more of the game than just watching the ball, check out the guards. If you can see the triangle of the guards and quarterback, that will give you a better insight. As you become more adept at following the action, you might even recognize the pass coverage. If there is a safety in the middle of the field, then there are probably three deep defenders and four underneath, so the quarterback will probably throw in an underneath zone. If the receivers are being covered tightly, then it is likely to be a man-to-man cover. You might just pick out one receiver to watch against the "man" defense. How does he try to get free? Does he hook? Does he start deep and then cut behind the defender? Does he try to just outrun him?

What to Watch For

On the snap of the ball, if the guards set up in pass protection, you can figure it will probably be a pass. Of course it could also be a draw play. So look downfield to see the patterns being run.

If the defense is dropping into zones, is it four underneath zones or five under zones? Remember that the quarterback and receivers are looking at the same defense you are seeing. With each defensive cue the receivers should make a complementary break, and the quarterback should anticipate their moves. In a recent Super Bowl game a receiver misread a coverage and made the wrong cut. The quarterback threw where he should have thrown, but the only player there was a defensive back who was ready for the interception and a touchdown. Later the receiver made the right read and cut, but the quarter-back made the wrong read and threw to the same defensive back. As you are reading the defensive coverage, can you see the openings?

Back to the guards. If the guards block forward and cross the line of scrimmage, you can switch your vision to the backs. Are they crossing or both going in the same direction? The crossing may be a key breaker to trick the linebackers. If the linebackers stay home, they are likely cross keying. But what if one or two guards pull right and the backs cross? If the backer stayed home, it would mean that he was only keying the back. If he followed the pull of the guards but ignored the opposite back, the coach might call for a play with a "false pull." In a false pull the guards would pull one way, but the ballcarrier would go the other way. We see this quite often in pro ball today.

You might want to watch the defensive linemen. How do they escape from a block, and how quickly do they pursue the ballcarrier? Since the defensive linemen can use their hands more than the offensive linemen can, watch what moves they make. Offensive linemen must keep their hands inside the shoulder-to-waist area of the defender, but defenders can use their hands on the outside of the blocker's body—on their elbows and shoulders. Do their hands get inside the blocker's hands? Coaches tell their players that "inside hands win."

There will be a lot of jersey holding. While technically it is a penalty, the pro officials disregard it, but college and high school officials will often call a holding penalty. You will notice that the jerseys are very tight. This is to reduce the ability of the opponents to hold. Game jerseys are commonly one or two sizes smaller than what the player would normally wear. But small jerseys are not the only defense against holding. A player may use double-sided adhesive tape on his shoulder pads. The tape will then hold the jersey tight to the pads. Or Velcro strips might be glued to the pads and sewn to the jersey to make an extra-tight fit. You have probably noticed in close-ups on TV that there are no loose sleeves. The sleeves are tight and short and tucked under the shoulder cup of the pad.

You might also want to watch a battle between an offensive lineman and a pass rusher. Here you should focus on the offensive left tackle, generally the best pass blocker, since he is protecting a right-handed passer's blind side. He is facing the man who is probably the defense's best pass rusher, their defensive right end. How deep does the tackle set? Is he protecting his inside?

Does the defender use a speed rush to the inside or outside? Does he club the blocker's shoulder hard with one hand, then use his other hand to "swim" over the blocker's shoulder or "rip" under it to get to the passer?

Watching the Special Teams

There is a lot to enjoy and analyze in the kicking game—the so-called special teams. Does the kickoff team do something to throw off the receiving team's blocking assignments? Most receiving teams will count the kickoff team from one side to the other, and the returners will each know which man they are assigned to block: the "one" man, the "four" man, and so on. But some kickoff teams will huddle around the ball and then break out quickly as the kicker approaches and kicks the ball. This may not give the receivers time to accurately count the tacklers, and missed assignments may accrue. Another method used to confuse the receiver's blocking is to cross two or three players. This is often done on the outside against teams that like to use a trapping return to either side. Still another method is to start one or two members of the kickoff team deep to give them a head start so they can reach full speed just as they reach the scrimmage line. This can throw off the timing of the blocking. But more than that, these "gunners" will hit different spots between their teammates, so they change the numbering just as the ball is kicked.

Watching the receiving team is usually more fun, but you can start with the kickoff team and then switch to the receiving team as the ball is kicked. Some teams will have most of their players block their men one direction, then have one or two blockers trap out on the potential tacklers. Usually this is done on the widest cover people, but sometimes it is done on an inside man. It is more common to have a four- or five-man wedge set up in front of the ball, start forward, and hope that they can create a hole in the cover team's line of tacklers. If so the ballcarrier might find a hole and get a good return. Sometimes the wedge fans out sideways hoping to screen off defenders, while other blockers take care of the tacklers to the inside of the swinging wedge.

The punt is also an interesting study. It is the most important play of the game. The punting team is concerned with two things—not getting the punt blocked, then not allowing a return. At the pro level only two people can release downfield before the ball is kicked. It is hoped that this will allow for more returns. At the high school and college levels all players can release downfield on the snap of the ball, but of course if they did there would be no one there to protect the kicking unit and many blocked punts.

So what is the happy medium? Let's look at the common pro punt. There are two split ends or gunners eager to get downfield and make the tackle. There are five linemen and two wingbacks, then a personal protector about four or four and a half yards behind the snapper. On the snap the line and wings take two steps back and then block. The quick two-step retreat allows them to see any crossing stunts by the defense that might allow a punt blocker to penetrate the line and have a shot at the block. If anybody does get through, the personal protector should get him. A disadvantage is that once the punt is made the linemen and wings are about a yard deeper than they would have been if they hadn't retreated.

Now for the pro punt return. Since the snap is almost always perfect, pros don't look for the punt block as often as high school and college teams do. Instead, they usually use two players on each of the punt team's gunners, trying to delay their progress so their punt returner has a chance to catch the ball and get going in the open field. They will normally try to get one player into the punter's backfield to ensure that the ball is kicked. If no one rushes the punter, he can hold the ball and give his coverage people another second or two to get downfield. The snap should get back to the punter in less than 0.8 second, and he will take about 1.2 seconds to get the punt off. The punt should be high to give the cover people time to get downfield. The "hang time" of a punt should be about a tenth of a second for every yard the punt travels past the line of scrimmage. So a 45-yard punt should have a hang time of four and a half seconds. The total time of the snap, punt, and hang time will give the gunners about six and a half seconds to sprint 45 yards—a distance they should be able to run in less than five seconds. If the defenders can delay the gunners for two to two and a half seconds, the returner has a chance to get moving.

What to Watch For

When watching the punt you might concentrate on the gunner. See how he is being delayed and what he does to avoid being delayed. You might also check the defensive linemen to see how they set up for the return. Do they all move to one side of the field trying to set up a "picket," a picket fence behind which the returner can run?

At the college and high school levels, some teams will use the pro punt, but many will use a punt formation that allows for better and quicker coverage. Many use an older formation from the 1950s with seven linemen, possibly the ends split, and three blockers back about five yards. The linemen may block for one or two seconds and then release in coverage. The deep three blockers should be able to pick up any leakage, but they will be slow in the coverage. Watch first for potential punt blockers. Versus a three-deep blocker set there will probably be two punt rushers challenging one of the outside blockers— one going inside and one outside. But the punt block isn't used as much as it should be at the lower levels of play. (Frank Beamer at Virginia Tech is a major exception. His teams block several punts every season.)

Back to the punt return. Since this is what you will see most often, check which offensive linemen are being held up, then where the defenders go for the punt return. As just mentioned they will usually set a picket to one side, but sometimes if the punt team players take wide lanes in their coverage the return team will set up a middle return with two lines about five yards apart in the middle of the field.

For the field goal or extra point, the offense must be concerned that the kick is not blocked. They also must be ready to fake a kick and run or pass for the score. The defense must put some rush on the kick and try to get a hand on it. It also must protect against a fake. Many teams today will try to get their defensive line to push hard on the offensive guards, moving them back a yard or two, then have a tall jumper come in behind and leap high, trying to get a hand on the ball. Other teams will try to attack between the wingback and end, putting a man on the end, then one inside and one outside the wing, hoping he can block only one kick blocker.

Pick up the keys that the coaches are looking for. Has the offensive coach sent in extra receivers? Did the defensive coach send in extra defensive backs to counter that offensive strength? Do the receivers always line up at the same width from the linemen, or do they adjust their splits depending on whether they are going to cut inside or outside? Do the defensive ends rush wide enough to contain the passer, or might he circle the ends or bootleg to gain extra time on a pass?

If you want to see the game through a coach's eyes, there is much more to watch than simply who has the ball!

CHAPTER 17
Playing and Coaching Flag and Touch Football

◆◆◆◆◆◆◆◆◆◆◆◆◆◆◆◆◆◆◆◆◆◆◆◆◆◆◆◆◆◆◆◆◆◆◆◆

Flag and touch football are played by far more people than the tackle version of the game. With the popularity of the tackle game, it wasn't long before boys began to play it in the streets and parks. Whether it was the abrasive surface of the playing field, the varying sizes of the boys, or the desire to keep their bodies unscathed, we will never know. But soon touching instead of tackling became a common game. With variations ranging from two hands below the waist, two hands anywhere, or one hand anywhere to replace the tackle, you can imagine the arguments that ensued—"I gotcha." "No you didn't." Sometime around the 1940s someone had the idea of tucking two-foot-long narrow rags into the pants—then when the flag was pulled it eliminated the arguments. But lo, American ingenuity being what it is, some enterprising but less than honest young men tied the flags to their jockstraps and scored a lot of touchdowns.

But again, American ingenuity saved the day. Belts were produced with a flag on each hip, and some with a flag over the tailbone, attached to the belt with suction cups, Velcro, or other adhesives. With a few rules that prevented the player from protecting the flag with the hand or arm, we developed an almost foolproof argument reducer. This gave rise to the birth of a large number of male, female, and coed leagues as the game became more popular.

Flag football is now played in many countries, and the Americans are not always dominant. The American men have won five of the last eight international championships, with Mexico, Canada, and France all winning one. The American women have won one women's championship, and the women of Mexico have won six, with Canada and France each taking a gold as well. The

NFL has also sponsored and conducted world championships for youth teams for both boys and girls. Championships have been played in Germany, China, Canada, Mexico, and Japan.

The Games of Flag or Touch

While male or female teams usually have seven players, coed teams often have eight. But teams of four to nine are all relatively common. And if the kids in the neighborhood are playing, there may only be two or three on a team. Another consideration is how much contact will be allowed. Some leagues allow no contact, some allow it only on the offensive side of the line of scrimmage, while some allow it all over the field.

A common field dimension is 80 yards long with two 10-yard end zones. This field might be the same width as a tackle field, 53⅓ yards. Other fields may be set crossways on a regulation field. Three or four fields set laterally across a regulation field would give field widths of 40 or 30 yards. If you are playing on the street, the curbs are the obvious sidelines. We used to play touch or tackle on the hard sand at the beach. One sideline would be the berm, the ledge where the sand slopes more steeply toward the water. The other sideline was China, so we ran and swam a lot!

In a league or at school, first downs are made by crossing a line parallel to the goal line. These lines are generally 20 yards apart. This works out fine on a 60-, 80-, or 100-yard field. On a 70-yard field the lines might be at the 15-yard lines and at midfield. When using these lines, you might find yourself with a first down on your 19-yard line. You would then have four downs to get one yard. If you gained two yards on the next play, you would now have a first down with 19 yards to go. If you had gained 11 yards, you would have had a first and 10. If you are playing on an unlined field, you might play that three complete passes, each over five yards, would give you a first down.

Equipment is regulated in the interest of safety and fairness. Jewelry is forbidden. You don't want to be cut by a ring or bracelet. And you don't want your earlobe ripped if somebody sticks his or finger in your hoop earring. Pants can't have belt loops or pockets because a finger missing the flag might find its way into a crevice and break, or worse, pull your pants off. No headgear with a hard surface, like the bill of a baseball cap, is allowed. No pads or braces are allowed above the waist, and if braces are worn on the legs, they must be adequately padded. Shoes may be required to have soft rubber soles, but some leagues will allow short rubber "soccer style" cleats.

The game length may be an hour, with four 15-minute quarters and a few minutes between quarters. Or if you are trying to schedule games starting on the hour, you may play two 22-minute halves. Running time is used in flag ball, but some leagues will use NCAA rules the last two minutes of the game, stopping the clock on incomplete passes or changes of possession. If the game is tied at the end there can be one or more overtime periods where each team gets four downs to score from the 10-yard line. Obviously, pickup games played on the street and in parks might have a less formal setup, agreed upon by the two teams before the start of play.

Scoring

Scoring follows the traditional rules of six points for a touchdown and two for a safety. Some leagues will add extra incentives for female players, giving an extra three points for a female throwing or catching a touchdown pass. Some leagues also allow for more point possibilities for conversions, such as one point from the 3-yard line, two points from the 10, and three points from the 20. Some will also give up to three points for a defensive conversion, such as intercepting a pass on a conversion attempt and returning it for a score.

Rules

The rules are intended to make the game as safe as possible, eliminate cheating, and yet allow the excitement of a wide-open football game to be experienced. But there are so many variables in the size and makeup of the teams, the size of the field, whether the game allows blocking, the scoring, and how first downs will be made that few leagues or games will use the exact same rules.

Kicking may or may not be allowed. Some leagues allow only a punt-type kick for all kicks—punts and kickoffs. Some leagues substitute touching the ball to the ground and then throwing it for a kick.

Another variation is the number of eligible pass receivers. Some leagues allow only ends and backs to catch forward passes, as in tackle football. In flag or touch football, as in tackle, all players can catch lateral passes. Some leagues allow all offensive players to be eligible pass receivers, some all but the snapper, the center.

Tackle Football Rules in Flag or Touch. Some rules are the same as in tackle football:

- Only the snapper can be in the neutral zone. Anyone else crossing the line of scrimmage is offside or encroaching.

- Only one player can be in motion when the ball is snapped. It must be a back, and the motion cannot be forward.

- There is no blocking in the back (clipping).

- If a receiver catches the ball near a sideline and then goes out of bounds, some leagues require that one foot has to touch the field of play after the catch, as in NCAA rules; some leagues require that both feet touch inbounds after the catch, as in pro rules.

Some rules are similar to, but more strictly enforced than tackle rules:

- For a seven-player offensive team, four must be on the line of scrimmage. For an eight-player team, five must be on the line.

- When an offensive or defensive player interferes with another's opportunity to make a catch by hitting the other rather than playing the ball, it is pass interference. Also if a player de-flags another before the catch it is pass interference. Tripping an opponent is not allowed.

Neutral zone: The area bounded by the two ends of the ball that extends from sideline to sideline and from the ground to the sky. Only the snapper can be in that zone before the ball is snapped.

Rules Strictly for Flag or Touch. Some rules are specific to flag or touch:

- A ballcarrier cannot protect the flag with hands, arms, shoulders, or the ball and must have the shirt tucked in so the flag is visible and not protected.

- A punt must be called by the offensive team. When a "protected" punt is called, the defense cannot rush the punter and the punting team members cannot cross the line of scrimmage until the ball is kicked.

- In non-contact games the offensive "blockers" can only stand in one place with their hands at their sides or behind them. They cannot move into a defender, they may only "screen" the defender from the ball.

- In "contact" games the offensive player can use the hands to block by putting them on the defender between the shoulders and waist. Some leagues allow such blocking only on the offensive side of the line of scrimmage, some allow it all over the field.

- Some games (especially pickup games with smaller groups) will regulate the pass rush with a verbal count, usually "Mississippis" (as in "One Mi-ssi-ssi-ppi, two Mi-ssi-ssi-ppi, etc.). The defender must count to an agreed-upon number of "Mississippis" before engaging the quarterback. Further, an agreed-upon number of blitzes are allowed for each set of downs (usually no more than two), where the defenders can run in prior to the full Mississippi count, provided they declare the blitz first. If it's third down and the defense hasn't blitzed yet, you should be expecting them to do so and plan accordingly.

- Fumbles and backward passes are dead if they hit the ground. They belong to the offensive team.

- Kickoffs that are not touched or are fumbled belong to the receiving team. A kickoff team cannot recover a ball after it has gone 10 yards, like an onside kick.

- Players cannot hold or tackle a ballcarrier or try to steal the ball.

Additional coed or co-rec rules include the following:

- A male cannot run the ball over the line of scrimmage or field a kick and run forward. He can run after catching a forward pass.

- Two possible rules exist to prevent male players from dominating the passing game. One is that after a male-to-male pass completion is made, the next completion must involve a female either as the passer or the receiver. The other possible rule is that only one male-to-male pass completion is allowed in any four-down series. Most coed leagues will use one of these rules. You may hear the terms "open plays" and "closed plays." An open play is one in which anyone can pass or catch the ball. A closed play is a play in which a male-to-male completion cannot be used.

Preparing to Play

Flag football can use many of the strategies and techniques discussed earlier. Like every sport, fundamentals are "fundamental." You can have intricate pass patterns perfectly executed, but if your passer can't throw the pass correctly or if the receiver can't catch the ball, it does no good. It is common to see young coaches designing intricate plays but not working on the fundamentals. You can use two or three minutes of practice time to have your team practice a pass play, and they might complete a single pass. If you use the same amount of time for a throwing and catching drill, you might easily get a throw and a catch every five to ten seconds. The skill level achieved by your players would undoubtedly be much greater running the drill.

As an illustration of the attention to the fundamentals of catching that is quite common among the pros, here is a drill that Hall of Famer Raymond Berry did every day. With a passer, often Johnny Unitas, he would run in place with his back to the passer, who was only about five yards away. Looking over his right shoulder, he would catch 10 soft passes high to his right, then 10 low to the right, then 10 low to his left where he would have to turn back toward the passer and reach down for the catch. Finally he would have 10 passes thrown high to his left. He would have to look away from the passer, look over his left shoulder to spot the ball, and catch it. So he caught 20 passes looking left, then 20 passes looking right. He did this daily throughout his All Pro career. Attention to detail and repetition is the secret for success in nearly every line of endeavor.

Here is a simple pass reception drill that should be done every practice. It helps both your offensive receivers and your linebackers and defensive backs. Three or four receivers get in a line about 20 yards from a passer. The first one jogs toward the passer, who throws the ball about chest high to the receiver. Catching the ball while running into it is a difficult skill. As the receivers get more proficient at catching, the passer passes the ball harder. Then he starts throwing it high or low and right or left. The catcher then puts the ball in the ball-carrying position while sprinting to the passer and returning the ball.

Players need to communicate with each other on defense, so the receivers should all yell "pass" when the passer raises the ball into the throwing position. When the ball is released, they all yell "ball." When the receiver thinks he can make the catch, he yells "got it," then when he catches it and has the ball tucked under his arm he yells the signal that the coach has chosen to indicate an interception—"Bingo" or "oskie" are commonly used. This is really a pass defense drill, but the catching skill is essential for the offensive players. Many coaches will have their receivers turn toward the ball on offense, then catch it at the highest point possible in its flight path. Also, this drill prepares your players to catch the ball in a hook pattern, which requires the receiver to turn around and then move back toward the passer. The hook pattern is the most effective pass pattern against a man-to-man defense, and it is highly effective against zone defenses as it gives the receiver the best chance to shake off a pursuing defender. For flag football the hook pattern is probably your most valuable pattern.

Hook pattern: A pass pattern in which the receiver runs downfield, stops, and then comes back toward the passer.

The reason for verbal communication is that if your defenders are playing man-to-man defense they will be looking at the offensive player, not the ball, so when they hear "pass" and "ball" they are alerted to the fact that the ball may be coming their way. If they hear "got it," they know the pass isn't coming their way, so they can release the receiver and go toward the ball because there is always a possibility that the ball will be tipped upward and another player might have the opportunity to catch it. If they are playing a zone defense, they should see the pass but won't be able to see the other defenders.

Defensively the players will need to be able to grab the flag effectively. If they are going to learn to do it they must practice it, just as tackle teams practice tackling daily.

Defensive Thoughts

In flag ball coaches or captains often forget about the effectiveness of a pass rush. They commonly use their slowest, poorest players to rush. If the passer is fast or a good athlete, he or she may be easily able to get outside the rusher and buy more time to throw. And the more time there is to throw, the better chance there is that receivers will break free and the pass will be complete.

Most flag defenses use man-to-man coverage. This certainly makes it easier to assign blame for a completed pass. If your players are much faster and much better athletes than the other team's, it should work just fine. In fact, everything you do should work fine. But if your players are less skilled players, a zone defense may be your best bet. Let's take a look at some simple ways to improve your man-to-man and zone play. If you are going to use both man and zone defenses, you may want to disguise them so they look the same to the offensive passer and receivers.

Three common alignments are used for man-to-man. One is right up on the line of scrimmage head up on a receiver. If your league is a contact league, this is an option, but it is not wise for non-contact leagues. This is a "bump and run" position. In this technique the players try to delay the receiver and throw the timing of the pattern off. It should give your rushers a bit more time to get to the passers. Just before the ball is snapped, a player can move to head up on the receiver's inside shoulder if the player has him alone and wants to force him outside, or move head up to the outside shoulder if the player wants to force the receiver inside and has inside help. The player should hit the receiver in the chest with the hand farthest from his nose and should move his or her feet quickly to stay in front of him as he tries to escape inside or outside. As the opponent starts to move past the defender, he or she should throw the other hand across his chest. This will help to turn the defender's body so that he or she can run with the receiver.

A second alignment is called "press" coverage. Here the players line up one to three yards deep and inside or outside a yard, depending on whether they have help inside or are on their own. The third alignment is 6 to 10 yards deep, usually a yard outside.

Whichever alignment the pass defender is in, he or she must watch the receiver to know when the ball is coming and where it is coming from. When the receiver looks for the ball it is a good indication that it will soon arrive. The pass defender should look at the receiver's eyes. They will get bigger when the ball is in sight. The defender should also be aware of where the receiver's hands are. They will go up when the ball is 10 to 15 feet away. If the defender is close and in a position to intercept, he or she can look and get both hands up. One caution: defenders cannot look at the receiver and put their hands up to obstruct his vision or maybe to be lucky enough that the ball will hit their hands. This is pass interference and is penalized.

Against man-to-man coverage, if it is to be a complete pass the ball must end up in the receiver's hands. It's no mystery. If the defensive player looks back for the ball it may fly right past him or her and find its way into the receiver's hands. But if the defender watches the hands and is close enough, he or she can get to the arm when the hands come up. You must drill on this. Pretty soon the good ballplayers will get to sense just when the ball will arrive. If they are very close and the receiver's hands go out they might look for the "pick."

Some college teams teach their defensive backs a technique to strip the receiver of the incoming ball. With the defender on the receiver's hip, as the receiver's hands go up to catch the ball and the defender sees "the flash of the ball" across his face the defender attacks the receiver's near arm by hitting it with either of his own arms.

Zone defense is easier to teach and can be played by lesser athletes. Assuming you have a seven-player team and you have two rushers, you can play three or four players in the short zones 5 to 15 yards deep and one or two in the deep zones. In a pure zone defense the defenders run to the middle of their zones as soon as they see a pass play emerging. Those in the short zones watch the eyes of the passer. If they can't see the eyes, they watch the nose. As soon as the passer looks downfield, all zones change with the quarterback's look.

There are two common techniques for the people in the short zones to use as the passer throws. One is to just sprint in the direction of the throw, adjusting the path as they see the height of the ball. This is the simplest method. The other is to glance at the receiver as they sprint in the direction of the passer's glance. They then adjust their run to position themselves in front of the receiver for a possible interception.

The one or two players in the deep zone must sprint back to the center of their zones. They should not be near a receiver. Any long pass will land 15 to 25 yards deeper than the receiver was when the pass was thrown. The deep backs are usually coached to keep getting depth in the middle of their zones until they see the "long arm" action of the passer. When a passer fakes a short pass it is usually a short arm movement, but to throw long the ball will generally be brought back behind the head. A better technique, if the passer doesn't "look off" the backs, is to have them sprint in the direction the passer looks. This can give them a 10- to 20-yard advantage over waiting for the "long arm" action of the passer.

Some Offensive Ideas

The passing game is generally the major weapon in flag or touch football. Some offensive techniques and tactics will work against either man or zone defenses. Versus man-to-man, the most commonly used flag and touch defense, double cut or crossing patterns are the most productive. A hook pattern is probably the most effective and the easiest to complete.

In a hook pattern the receiver runs upfield to the required distance—10 to 12 yards is common. The receiver plants the outside foot, turns inward, and comes back to the quarterback looking for a low pass. The passer watches the receiver, and as the receiver begins to slow and plants the foot the passer passes low, one to two feet above the ground, to a point two yards nearer than the receiver's foot plant.

When the defender has seen several hooks and begins to "jump" the pattern aggressively, the "hook and go" is called. One receiver must run a deep post pattern to draw the near deep defender deeper and toward the middle of the field. The hooking receiver will run about eight yards and hook, but not come back toward the passer. The passer makes a good fake toward the hooking receiver, then, without pausing, immediately throws the ball high and to the outside, about 7 to 10 yards wider than the hook and about 10 yards deeper. The receiver waits for the fake, then breaks outside and deep, looking over his outside shoulder.

Another individual pattern that is effective is a 10-yard out. The receiver works to get the defender to turn inside, then cuts about 100 degrees to the outside, working back to about an eight-yard depth. The pass is thrown low and in front of the receiver. The counter to this pattern is an "out and up." The pattern breaks at about eight yards and is a 90-degree cut. Like the hook and go, the passer fakes the pass on the first cut, then immediately throws deep over the receiver's inside shoulder. Another receiver must run deep through the safety's zone.

Another tactic is to cross receivers, either the two inside receivers or an inside and outside receiver on the same side. The pass should be to the closest receiver just as he or she is making the crossing pattern.

The possibilities are nearly endless.

Against a zone defense the hook pattern will work. Patterns against the zone defense are more likely to use two or three players against one or two defenders. Against linebackers you can put one receiver about 5 yards deep and a second one 15 to 18 yards deep. This would be called a vertical stretch. You can also put receivers inside and outside of a defender. This is called a horizontal stretch.

Vertical stretch: Forcing the pass defenders to cover the length of the field on a pass by sending at least one receiver deep.

Horizontal stretch: Forcing the pass defenders to cover the entire width of the field on a pass.

Just like in the pros, as a coach or captain you should know the defensive and offensive thinking and the potential of your opponents and develop a strategy to take advantage of their weaknesses.

CHAPTER 18
Coaching Youth Football

◆▬◆◆◆◆◆◆◆◆◆◆◆◆◆◆◆◆◆◆◆◆◆◆◆◆◆◆◆◆◆◆◆◆◆

At any level of coaching or teaching—and coaching is teaching—the coach will have a philosophy, a reason, for why he or she is coaching. And the player will have a philosophy of why he or she is playing. At the professional level the coach is hired to win. The professional players will be motivated by the public accolades they receive, by winning, by testing themselves against the best, and of course by the money. Money has become much more of a motivating factor at the professional level. But if you are a youth coach, you are coaching for yourself or for the children.

Why does an eight-year-old play flag football? Why does a twelve-year-old play tackle? Their answers would probably be, "because it is fun." But what is the coach's reason? Is it to win at any cost? Is it to be able to brag to his or her friends and neighbors about how well his or her team is doing? At the youth level the reason for coaching should be to teach the fundamentals and to conduct the practices so that they are fun.

If you are a parent, do you ask your children, "Did you win?" or do you ask, "Did you have fun?" The question you ask gives the child a whole different slant on what is success and what is the expected outcome of playing. And isn't "playing" done for enjoyment of the activity?

Because many youth coaches are not professional educators, as high school coaches usually are, there may be an uncompromising goal of winning, without the emphasis on life skills that should be the emphasis of the coach-teacher. This might be the time to reread Mike Singletary's message in the section titled "The Soul of the Game" in Chapter 3. Many former pro players and coaches refuse to let their children play youth league football because either they think that the game is being introduced too early or they are concerned about the ability of the youth coach to use the game as a tool of education. One former pro running back, a Hall of Famer and Olympic gold medal sprinter, didn't want his son to play youth football. He finally changed his mind because all his son's friends were playing, but he would only let him play in the line. His son eventually had great success as a college basketball player.

When I was in high school there were 910 boys in the school, and 550 went out for spring football, all in full uniform. In the fall the school fielded five teams of different weight classes. It was not uncommon then, with no youth football, to have varsity teams of 100 squad members. Today, in many areas, high school varsity teams are lucky to have 15 squad men, while the more successful programs may have well over 100 players out for the team. And in Texas, the haven and heaven for football desire, we know of one school that had six full freshmen teams working their way up to the varsity level. The school had 50 coaches. It is commonly said by high school coaches that the most supportive administrations and parents are in Texas and in Catholic schools!

In talking to many high school coaches we find that while youth football can keep quarterbacks and wide receivers motivated to continue, many offensive linemen have had enough. And there are more competing interests today than ever before to beckon and distract many potential athletes. The point is that youth coaches need to see the larger picture. A yelling and screaming coach of 10-year-olds may be pushing some of his players to the unchallenging world of video games and Internet surfing. They may be turning some of their charges away from the potentially valuable experiences that are common in high school football.

Motivation

Psychologists, and this includes sport psychologists, tell us that the best way to motivate people is through positive encouragement. Naturally when a player does something wrong you can't compliment him on it, so how can you make your input positive? Well, first find something positive to say to get his attention: "Your stance was good." Then make the corrections: "But you stepped with the front foot first rather than the back foot." Then come back with something positive: "Remember that on this block you step at a 45-degree angle with your rear foot. I know you can do it."

Traditionally when teachers or coaches haven't taught something effectively they have blamed the student. We wonder if the yelling coaches ever played or if they just had incompetent coaches themselves. Or maybe they have seen too many B movies about coaches made by directors who have never seen an effective coach. Anyone who has seen a modern college or pro football practice knows that most coaches are very positive. They may occasionally yell at a player for making a mistake consistently. But that player probably won't step on the grass in next weekend's game.

Sport psychologists tell us that there are two general motivations that move athletes. One is mastery, the other is ego involvement. Many students and adults are quite satisfied when they master a task—when they learn to multiply, when they learn to catch a football, when they learn to master Windows on their computer. Others are ego involved. They are primarily concerned with winning—being the first to learn to multiply, scoring a touchdown, being the first to own a computer. Americans tend to be ego involved. But people are more likely to experience satisfaction when they have mastered a skill or learned a concept. If winning is the only thing that is important, half of the people who play each game of football are failures. Anyone who has applied for a job and didn't get it is a failure. Anyone not asked to the senior prom is a failure.

Intelligent parents and coaches will work to develop the "mastery" component of learning and competition. Did the player on the losing team play better this week than last? Is the unsuccessful job seeker still a competent and employable person? Is the person not asked to the prom still a worthwhile person? What about the other side of the coin? Did the winning quarterback or right guard play less effectively than last week? Was the winning all-important, or is improvement more important?

Another motivational factor not to be overlooked is fun. If an eight-year-old had fun playing in his flag football game but lost—is he a failure? Because some parents and coaches are ego motivated, the child may see himself as a failure. Was the play in the eight-year-old's flag game for the fun of the participants or for the ego satisfaction of some nonplaying adults?

Theory

As mentioned in earlier chapters, there are three parts to the game: offense, defense, and kicking. Generally if you win two of these you will win the game. Within each of these areas there are subareas, like reducing penalties and increasing the turnover ratio. One principle used by most coaches is the "KISS" principle, variously translated as "Keep It Sound and Simple" or "Keep It Simple, Stupid." Many successful high school teams will have only four running plays and three or four passing plays in a game. A few years ago a team that went to the state finals in a Midwest state had thrown only six passes all year!

The point is that it isn't what you as a coach know, it's what the players know that matters. And what they know should be done as close to perfection as possible. Coaches call this "execution." I've seen flag football coaches of an eight-year-old team with elaborate playbooks. But Super Bowl–winning coach Bill Walsh stopped using playbooks for his 49er players, keeping them only for the coaches. Coaches may be able to use playbooks to make certain that they have the total picture, but they must be able to teach the part of the playbook that the players will need next week—and little should change from week to week for the players.

At every level of football, the running game is primary for the offense and the run defense is the most important aspect of defense. How will you make these happen with the material you have? Are you lucky enough to have a big, fast, indestructible do-everything running back? If so, lucky you. Are all your runners little and slow? If so, how do you prevent the season that never ends?

If you are coaching a tackle team, many of the fundamentals you might teach and the offensive and defensive theories you might use are discussed in our book *Coaching Football* (revised edition, McGraw-Hill, 2006). Most bookstores carry it on their shelves, and if it isn't on the shelves it can be ordered through Amazon.com. If you want to know more about offensive line fundamentals, get the book *Playing the Offensive Line* (Karl Nelson and Bob O'Connor, McGraw-Hill, 2006). While these books are designed for high school coaches, you can read about the fundamentals that you might need at any level.

Whatever you do, keep it simple. We are reminded of two Southern California coaches who changed their offenses weekly. The high school coach was an engineer who hadn't spent much time learning about the game. He thought the Xs and Os were what the game was about. The other coach was coaching at Cal Tech, the California Institute of Technology, one of the world's best scientific and engineering schools. He had been the head coach at UCLA, so he knew a bit about the game. His reasoning was that he didn't have good football players, but they were incredibly smart. They could easily learn a new offense and defense every week. Neither of them won any games, but they all had fun!

But back to your youth team. Evaluate your players. Teach them fundamentals. Concentrate on a simple defense that stops wide runs and reverses. Use a zone defense. Teach your players to tackle well, and practice it at every practice. Teach them how to steal the ball and how to recover fumbles. The younger the team, the more mistakes the players will make. Spend time learning to capitalize on the offense's mistakes. Teach your players to intercept passes, recover fumbles, and avoid penalties. Work your defensive line on staying onside. They must concentrate on the ball, not on the sound of the quarterback's signals. Drill them on tackling low so they don't touch the face mask.

Here is a simple drill that combines conditioning and staying onside on both offense and defense. Line up the players on a yard line. Have a quarterback call the signals, changing the snap count. The team sprints on the proper sound. When they have run their 20-, 30-, or 40-yard sprint, the team lines up on a near yard line. Here a coach with a ball on the ground calls out different types of signals that the team might hear—"hut, hut, hut" or "hu-to, hu-to" or "hike, hike, hike," but the team doesn't sprint until the coach moves the ball. So they should learn to go on sound on offense and on ball movement on defense. This is a simple way to reduce encroachment penalties.

The Raiders, in their Super Bowl game against Tampa Bay, had several defensive offside penalties that helped Tampa maintain drives. No matter what the level of play, a coach must work to reduce the most inexcusable of all penalties—encroachment.

For the kicking game, practice the punt every practice. No other play averages as many yards or has the defensive opportunities for scoring that the punt has. Work the long snapper before or after practice. Give him exercises to strengthen the muscles in the back of the upper arm (triceps) and the upper back (latissimus dorsi). Have him work with a parent or another player. The snapper reaches high with his hands together, and the helper puts his or her hands under the snapper's hands. The snapper then pushes downward against the resistance. If he goes to a gym, have him do straight-arm pulldowns on the lat machine. The best exercise is done on a low pulley. With a parent or helper holding his hips, while he is in the snapping position, he brings the pulley handle from far in front all the way to the crotch. This is the best exercise because he will be in the same posture he will use in a game. Recent research shows that exercising a muscle in the exact posture in which you will use the strength in the activity gives the most functional strength. Also, it is not just maximal strength that is important, but maximum power. Power comes from exercising as fast as possible with about 30 percent of one's "one repetition maximum" strength.

 Long snapper: The player who snaps the ball 7 or 8 yards to the holder of a placekick or 10 to 15 yards to a punter.

For offensive play, just adapt your formations and your attack to your material, keeping the number of formations and plays to a minimum. The aforementioned book, *Coaching Football*, will give you a number of ideas for formations and plays. Just don't be limited to what you see on television. The teams you see there have very different potentials than your team has.

The game of football must hold more fascination and joy than the electronic screens that tempt our youth with uncompetitive fantasies. The goalless pursuit of a narcotic nirvana or of sex doesn't build the strong character or the feeling of accomplishment that a well-run, educationally oriented football program can build.

Youth coaches must see their role as teachers of positive values that will make their players more complete people. Your legacy in the lives of your players will be the lessons of cooperation and fair competition, the satisfaction of accomplishment, the use of one's intelligence in meeting the challenges of the game, and the joy of play. In 20 years, how many parents will remember the score of their 12-year-old's September 12th game? In 20 years, how many of your former players will remember, positively or negatively, the lessons they learned because they played for you? We are reminded of the indelible words of the legendary sportswriter Grantland Rice: "For when the One Great Scorer comes to mark against your name, He writes—not that you won or lost—but how you played the Game." This applies to coaches even more than to players because it is the coaches who teach the players how to play the game. As a coach, just as a teacher, you never know how many generations you will influence with your actions of today and tomorrow.

CHAPTER 19
Playing Fantasy Football

◆▬◆▬◆▬◆▬◆▬◆▬◆▬◆▬◆▬◆▬◆▬◆▬◆

Fantasy football has taken the country by storm. Participating gives you the opportunity to select and manage your own professional team. So if you want to have a greater stake in the weekly NFL games, look into fantasy football. People who had little interest in the NFL have become addicts—after all, the players are playing for them. It's more fun than you can imagine.

First you will join a league. If there is already a league of your friends, relatives, or coworkers, you may be able to join it. Or you can start your own league. The other option is to join a public league and play against people from anyplace in the world. You may make some new friends. You can draft your own players, or you can let the host computer found on sites such as the NFL, Fox, Yahoo, or ESPN site draft for you. Your offensive team will include those players who can score—by running, passing, receiving, or kicking. One or two of your "players" will be a whole NFL defensive team. In reality your players will actually be playing for several different NFL teams, but whatever they do well will gain your team points. It is like having your own all-star team playing for you every week.

Every week of the NFL season you will start seven players and a kicker, as well as a defensive team if your league uses one—as most leagues do. You will choose players you think will perform well in their actual games. So your lineups will change somewhat from week to week. You will play an opponent from your league who will be doing the same thing.

Depending on your league rules, you can determine the winner of your league at the end of the league season, or you can take the best teams and have a playoff with a Super Bowl championship at the culmination of the season. If you are in a private or custom league you can make up your own rules, scoring system, roster limits, and so on. If you are in a public league the rules will be set for you.

Getting into a League

There are several major sponsors of fantasy football. The NFL, ESPN, and Yahoo are major players. Each has a different time period for sign-ups. Yahoo may let you sign up as late as mid-October, but sign-ups may start as early as June. You will need a commissioner to interpret and enforce the rules. If you play with a group of friends, just choose someone you trust. To get into a custom league, you will need a league ID and a password. These will be provided by the commissioner. With a custom league you can select your own scoring system and draft rules, and you will be among friends. You may even decide to charge an entry fee and give out prizes at the end of the season, or perhaps you might have a season-ending banquet.

You will need to set a league schedule and a playoff format, if you decide to have playoffs at season's end. For a non-playoff league a 16-team league is ideal because you will play a game during every week of the NFL season. With eight teams you can play every team twice. With a 10-team league, you might use two five-team divisions. The NFL fantasy program suggests a 12-team league, which makes it easier to have playoffs.

Let's assume that you want to use the NFL program. Go to the NFL.com/ fantasy Web page. Sign up to create an account and get your ID and password. If you are in a custom league, you would choose the League Manager type of game. If you want to be in a public league, you would let the provider choose a league for you. If you are in an NFL public or fantasy league, the game uses the NFL's basic scoring system, which awards six points for each touchdown, one point for every 25 passing yards, one point for every 10 rushing yards and receiving yards, and one point for defensive statistics such as touchdown returns, fumble recoveries, sacks, interceptions, safeties, and yards allowed.

Setting League Rules

As a league member, you can follow the rules commonly adhered to by your host site, or you can modify them.

1. Set the size of the roster—14 to 17 players is common.

2. Will there be penalties, such as point deductions, when "free agents" are added to a roster?

3. When will the league season start, and when will the playoffs start?

Setting How the Scoring Will Be Determined

Here is the NFL's fantasy scoring program:

Offense

- Offensive touchdown: 6 points

- Field goal: 3 points (if 49 yards or less), 5 points if 50 or more yards

- Kicking conversion: 1 point

- Running or passing conversion: 2 points

- Quarterback: 1 point for every 25 yards passing

- Receivers: 1 point for every 10 yards of receptions

- Runners: 1 point for every 10 yards

(Runners and receivers must complete the 10-yard increment for the point. So 19 running yards is not 1.9 or 2 points, only 1 measly point.)

Deducted points:

- Interception or fumble lost: -2

Defense

- Defensive or special team touchdown: 6 points
- Safety: 2 points
- Interception or fumble recovered: 2 points
- Quarterback sack: 1 point

Points scored against your defense in the game:

- 0 to 6 points allowed: 8 points for defense
- 7 to 13 points allowed: 6 points
- 14 to 20 points allowed: 4 points
- 21 to 27 points allowed: 2 points
- 28 or more points allowed: 0 points

Yards allowed by your defense in the game:

- Less than 49 yards allowed: 12 points for defense
- 50 to 99 yards allowed: 10 points
- 100 to 149 yards allowed: 8 points
- 150 to 199 yards allowed: 6 points
- 200 to 249 yards allowed: 4 points
- 250 to 299 yards allowed: 2 points
- 300 or more yards allowed: 0 points

ESPN uses a different scoring method. It has more options for kickers to score or be penalized.

ESPN Scoring

- Long field goal more than 50 yards: 5 points
- Long field goal 40 to 49 yards: 4 points

- Long field goal miss: -1

- Short field goal less than 39 yards: 3 points

- Short field goal miss: -2 points

If you are in a custom league you might set quite different rules. A touchdown is commonly six points, but some leagues will divide the points between the players who were involved, so a quarterback who threw a touchdown pass might get two or three points and the receiver three or four. Or each might be awarded six points. A running touchdown would be six points for the runner.

Bonus points might also be awarded. So a runner having a 100-yard game might get another three or six points, plus a point for every 10 yards he gained. A passer might be given bonus points for a 100-, 200- or 300-yard game.

Drafting the Players for Your Team

There are several different draft options available to managers.

You may choose to participate in a live online draft, where each manager selects a squad in real time. Every team selects one player per round until its roster is full. The draft order reverses each round, so the team that starts the first round will end the second, and the team that ends the first round will start the second.

You can opt for an autopick draft, and the computers will select your team. But the computer may choose different positions than you would choose. The computer might choose two defensive teams and one kicker, while you would prefer one defense and two kickers, or it might choose three running backs while you wanted four. But you can correct these problems by trades, selecting free agents, or picking up players on waivers.

If you have the time, it is more fun to do the live draft.

The Draft

In fantasy football the common method is to draw lots for the draft order. But the second round's first pick goes to the team that picked last in the first round. This order and reverse order, called a serpentine order, would continue until all the players are selected, 14 rounds for a 14-man maximum squad or 17 rounds for a 17-man maximum squad.

Another way to run a draft would be to determine a budget or a salary cap for each team in the league. Player names are either drawn out of a hat or nominated and auctioned off. If the cap is $100, for example, you could bid any part of that for a player. But if you bid $50 for Tom Brady, for example, you would only have $50 left for the rest of your team. You might have a chance to get some real stars, but it might hurt your team's depth. What if you bid a lot for Tom Brady in 2008, but his injury kept him out for the season?

Since players in the NFL often sustain injuries, you will need more than one player at each position. Also, each NFL team will have a bye week, so the players on that team will not score for fantasy teams; consequently you need backups for your starters. You might choose two or three quarterbacks, two tight ends, one or two kickers, and four or five running backs and wide receivers. If you are in a league that uses a defense and scores defensive points, you will also want one or two defensive teams.

For each game most leagues allow you to start seven players—a quarterback, two running backs, two wide receivers, a tight end, and a kicker—along with a defense. Your league may require you to start one quarterback, one tight end, one kicker, one defense, two running backs, and two wide receivers. Or you may be able to start three wide receivers, dropping your tight end or a running back. It is common to set a maximum number of starters at each position: one quarterback, one kicker, one tight end, two running backs, and three wideouts and only one defensive team. Your strategy in the draft might be to draft no tight ends (whose usefulness to their team in terms of blocking won't help your fantasy stats) and to stock up on wide receivers.

If you participate in a live draft, you can select based on your needs and prejudices. If a computer selects for you, you may or may not be able to tell the computer exactly the type of players you want.

Drafting a Competitive Team

When you draft, you must have a clear idea of the scoring system your league will use. Will the quarterback get six or fewer points for a touchdown pass? Will a running back get points only for scoring, or will he also get points for total yardage? Will a quarterback be your first choice? He will be involved in much of the scoring. Is he playing for a team that relies a great deal on the pass? If so, he has more chances of scoring points for you. But if you are in a league that gives only three points to the quarterback for a passing touchdown, he may not be worth an early draft pick.

Running backs are generally considered to be the bread and butter of a fantasy team because while each NFL team has one premier running back, but each fantasy team uses two backs every week. Because of this you will want at least three and possibly five running backs. Wide receivers, particularly the big play guys or the possession-type receivers, may rate fairly high. In leagues that allow you to play three wideouts and no tight end, you might use up to five draft choices here.

Selecting your draftees based on their probable value as point getters is an intelligent approach, but it requires a great deal of knowledge about their past seasons, and maybe some insights from the NFL preseason games. Then you can make your own, hopefully educated, guesses on their fantasy point production for the upcoming season. You will then rank each position according to your educated guesses.

You might base your values on the player's performance last year or the last two years, or you might predict next year's point production. If a receiver is traded to a team with a better quarterback and a better pass protecting line, he might be much more productive than he was last year. A few years ago Randy Moss was unproductive with Oakland; the next year he was a phenomenon with the Patriots. Or there may be a "can't miss" college player coming into the league like Adrian Peterson or Barry Sanders.

If you are in it just for fun, you may take some of your favorite players, or take more players from your favorite team. Sometimes drafting from your heart instead of your head works out just fine. What if several years ago you were a real NFL coach and chose a quarterback just because he went to Michigan or because he had played in the same Northern California Catholic high school league that you played in? You might have picked Tom Brady earlier than the sixth round. Our favorite story about picking a player on a prejudice had sport psychologist Dr. Blake Miller choosing, as his first draft pick in 1999, a backup quarterback who had just signed with the Rams as a free agent. Blake had played against him when he was a backup junior quarterback at Northern Iowa and Blake was a linebacker for Augustana. Drafting from the heart won Blake his fantasy league championship that year because his ridiculous pick—

of Kurt Warner—brought the Rams to the Super Bowl and won it, with Kurt as the Super Bowl MVP.

Draft Strategies

If you are going to do your own picking in the draft, rather than letting the computer draft for you, you will make out lists for every position with the players who might be drafted, how you rate them, and their bye weeks. You certainly don't want two quarterbacks or kickers with the same bye week!

Running backs are a high priority for fantasy football. With 32 NFL teams, that gives you 32 running backs. Some teams will alternate running backs. That makes each one less of a scorer for fantasy ball. Fullbacks usually block, so they are not a high priority. If you are in a 12-team league, there will be 24 running backs playing for your league every week. Two of the 32 backs will be sitting out in a bye week. So only 30 NFL backs will start in a real NFL game every week. But only 12 of the NFL's 32 quarterbacks will start in your league each week. Fantasy owners will often take two running backs in the first two rounds and maybe three in the first four rounds. With a 12-team league there are only enough starting tailbacks to give every team about two and a half running backs, and each one will miss a game. Another factor in choosing your running backs is whether their teams have bye weeks at the end of the season when your team may be in the playoffs and would need your most productive players.

In the real games, touchdown passes are often spread around to different receivers, so with a few exceptions wideouts are generally not as valuable as running backs. In leagues that give points for each reception or for reception yardage wide receivers become more valuable.

Many experienced fantasy footballers take an approach something like this: they draft two running backs in the first two rounds, then a wide receiver, then a quarterback or another receiver. If yours is a team that gives defensive points, a defensive team might fit in next. An outstanding placekicker could fit in around here also. Then you could fill out the draft picks with productive tight ends, running backs, another quarterback, and some more wide receivers. Since there are bye weeks, you will probably want two kickers, otherwise on your kicker's bye week you won't get any points. However you could pick up a free agent when your kicker is sitting out. Bye weeks are a reason to have players from several teams. If you choose eight Cowboys because you are a Dallas fan, you may be in big trouble when the Cowboys aren't playing!

Adding and Dropping Players

The draft is merely the starting point for developing your squad. One of your players may be injured or not playing as well as you would prefer. You can trade him, if anybody wants him, or put him on waivers. You can then pick up another player who is on waivers or is an undrafted free agent.

Waivers

When a previously active player is no longer wanted, he is placed on waivers. Any team can claim him. It's safe to assume that most players on waivers (except for the injured) would be superior to the free agents who were not drafted. If more than one team wants to claim a player, the order of preference will be set by the league rules. If the waiver is done soon after the draft, it is common to let the team that drafted latest have the first pick. During the season, the team with the poorest win percentage or the team that has scored the fewest points may have the first pick. Anyone who isn't drafted in your league is a free agent and can be added to your team. But if you pick up an extra player your roster has to be back to its league-mandated maximum or fewer by the next game.

Owners can trade players with other owners—one for one or maybe even three for one. Your league may have a trade deadline that stops all trading for the season. An approval may be required for the trade. If your sister's team is doing well but your team doesn't have a shot at the playoffs, it wouldn't be ethical for you to trade your big point scorers to her, taking her least effective players. Sibling rivalry notwithstanding, you may have even agreed to split the prize if she wins. Heaven forbid!

Schedule

Every team should play every other team at least once. With a 10-team league you could have two divisions. Every team would play each other team once and every team in their division once more, a total of 13 games. The top four teams can be selected for the playoffs, with the best team playing the fourth-best team and the second and third playing each other in the semifinal. Then comes your Super Bowl. The fantasy Super Bowl must take place before the end of the NFL league games. Because not all NFL players are on teams that make the NFL playoffs, if your season lasted into the NFL playoffs some players wouldn't be able to score. Your league can be tracked with special software, or the previously mentioned Internet services will do it for you.

Each week you will choose your playing team of two running backs, a quarterback, a tight end, two wide receivers, a kicker, and a defensive unit if your league uses defense. You must keep abreast of the weekly injury reports. If you choose to start a player who is injured and can't play for his real team, he can't score any points for you. If a player has been suspended or demoted, he won't do you any good either. Maybe your best wide receiver will be facing the league's best defensive back or the league-leading pass defense this week. But what if one of your lower-ranked receivers is playing a team where the starting cornerbacks are either injured or are not much of a match for this receiver? He may be able to get you some points. Maybe your best running back is facing the league's best run defense on the field, but your fourth-best back is playing against the league's weakest defense. It's a no-brainer who you start! And don't forget, if your favored running back or quarterback is playing behind an offensive line that has a starter or two out with injuries, he may not perform very well this week.

Contacting Providers

Two major providers of fantasy football are the NFL (NFL.com/fantasy/fantasy101) and Yahoo (http://football.fantasysports.yahoo.com). Another league run by USA Today has created a very simple way to play the fantasy game. You don't need a league, a draft, or anybody else to play—it's free and there are prizes! Every week you will play against a former NFL player. You choose just three players: a quarterback, a running back, and a wide receiver—

the three players that you think will put up big numbers this week. It couldn't be simpler. Just log on to usatoday.com and check its fantasy site.

You can keep updated on fantasy football by following the game providers, such as NFL, Fox, Yahoo, and ESPN, and by reading the seasonal magazines devoted to the game. You can find them at your local newsstand or at Amazon.com. The more popular magazines are the following:

- *Fantasy Football.com*
- *Fantasy Football Index*
- *NFL Fantasy Football*
- *Fantasy Football*
- *Lindy's Fantasy Football*
- *Fantasy Football—Preview Issue*
- *NFL.Com Fantasy Football Preview*

Epilogue

The more you know, the more interesting any activity becomes. Whether it is history, politics, golf, or football—the more you know, the more questions you have and the more you want to know. "Knowledge is power," as Francis Bacon once wrote. And we add, "Knowledge provides enjoyment." The more you know about this sport and the games that have sprung from it, the more enjoyable your watching, coaching, playing, or fantasy games will be. After all, football may be the greatest game ever devised!

Glossary of Common Football Terms

◆◆◆◆◆◆◆◆◆◆◆◆◆◆◆◆◆◆◆◆◆◆◆◆◆◆◆◆◆◆

Audible: Calling the offensive play at the line of scrimmage.

Backpedal: Running directly backward, a technique used by defensive backs and linebackers.

Blitz: A defensive play in which a linebacker or defensive back attacks past the line of scrimmage.

Boot or bootleg: The quarterback fakes one way to backs while he goes the opposite way to run or pass.

Box: An area that coaches and quarterbacks check in the defense to see how strong the defense might be against the run. It is an area from a yard or two outside the offensive tackles and to a depth of six or eight yards. The area is inexact and varies from coach to coach.

Bump and run: A technique in which the defensive back hits the potential receiver on the line of scrimmage (to slow his route) and then runs with the receiver.

Choice route: A receiver runs to a certain point and then has several choices of patterns depending on the directions that the pass defenders move.

Clip: A block in which the defender is hit from behind. It is illegal.

Counter: A play that ends going in a different direction than the initial flow of the backs would indicate.

Curl: A pass pattern in which the receiver runs 12 to 20 yards downfield and then comes back toward the passer in an open area of the defensive coverage.

Cutback: The movement of a ballcarrier away from the direction he was originally running so that he can run behind the tacklers.

Dive: A quick straight-ahead play with the halfback carrying the ball.

Dog or red dog: A linebacker attacking past the line of scrimmage at the snap of the ball.

Down: A play that begins after the ball is stopped. There are two types of downs, a scrimmage down and a free-kick down.

Drag: A delayed pattern in which a tight end or a wideout runs a shallow pattern across the center.

Draw: A fake pass that ends with one of the backs carrying the ball after the defensive linemen are drawn in on the pass rush.

Encroachment: Entering the neutral zone (the line of scrimmage bounded by the two ends of the ball) before the ball is snapped. It is a penalty in high school football. At the college and pro level it is a penalty only if contact is made with the other team.

End around: A reverse play in which a tight end or a wideout carries the ball.

Fade: A pass pattern used generally against a man-to-man coverage in which the receiver runs deep and fades away from the defender.

Fair catch: The opportunity for a receiving player to catch a kicked ball and not be tackled. It is signaled by waving one arm overhead. The ball cannot be advanced after making a fair catch.

Field goal: A ball placekicked or drop-kicked over the goalposts. It scores three points.

Flanker: A back split wider than a wingback.

Flow: The apparent direction of the ball during a scrimmage play. Most plays attack in the direction of the flow. Counters, reverses, and throwback passes go against the flow.

Free safety: The safetyman opposite the power side of the offensive line (the tight end). He is usually free to cover deep zones.

Freeze option: A play in which an inside fake to one back running up the middle should freeze the linebackers. The play then becomes an option play between the quarterback and another runner.

Front: The alignment of the defensive linemen.

Game plan: The offensive, defensive, and kicking strategy against an opponent.

Guards: The offensive linemen on either side of the center.

Hang time: The amount of time a kick stays in the air.

Hash marks: Short lines parallel with the sidelines that intersect each five-yard mark on the field. For high school the hash marks are a third of the field in, 53⅓ feet. For college they are 60 feet in, and for the pros 70¾ feet.

H-back: An all-purpose back who may be used as a tight or wide receiver or may carry the ball, especially on countering plays.

Hitch: A quick pattern to a wide receiver in which he drives off the line and then stops.

Hook pattern: A pass pattern in which the receiver runs downfield, stops, and then comes back toward the passer.

Horizontal stretch: Forcing the pass defenders to cover the entire width of the field on a pass.

Hot receiver: A receiver who becomes open because the defender who would have covered him has stunted into the offensive backfield.

I formation: A formation in which the quarterback, fullback, and tailback are in a line.

Influence: Getting an opponent to move in the direction desired through finesse.

Jam: Hitting a potential receiver before the ball is released by the passer. It may also mean the position of the pass defender on a wideout, either up on the line or back two yards.

Key: Watching an opponent to determine what he or his team will be doing.

Lateral pass: A pass thrown parallel with the line of scrimmage or backward. It can be thrown overhand or underhand.

Line of scrimmage: An area approximately a foot wide (the width of the ball) that stretches from sideline to sideline.

Long snapper: The player who snaps the ball 7 or 8 yards to the holder of a placekick or 10 to 15 yards to a punter.

Loop: A defensive lineman's move from a gap to a gap or man to a man.

LOS: Line of scrimmage.

Matchup zone: A zone coverage in which the defenders are responsible to play man-to-man on various receivers, depending on the receiver's route.

Mike: Middle guard or nose man (Mike means "middle in"), the term used by many coaches to name the middle linebacker.

Misdirection: A play that goes against the flow of the play, such as a bootleg, reverse, or throwback.

Muff: A mistake in catching the ball on a kicking play.

Neutral zone: The area bounded by the two ends of the ball that extends from sideline to sideline and from the ground to the sky. Only the snapper can be in that zone before the ball is snapped.

Nickel defense: A defense with five defensive backs.

Nose guard or nose tackle: A defensive lineman playing on the offensive center.

Odd defense: A defense that has a man on the offensive snapper. This will result in a defensive line with an odd number of players on it.

Offset: A player lines up in a slightly different spot, such as a fullback lining up behind a guard or tackle, or a defensive lineman or linebacker lining up a half man or a man laterally, such as a nose tackle lining up on the side of the offensive center rather than being directly head up.

Onside kick: A short kickoff that travels at least 10 yards, which can then be recovered by either team.

Option play: A play in which the quarterback runs at a wide defender, forcing the defender to either tackle him or stop the pitch to a trailing back. The quarterback can keep or pitch.

Overshift: The alignment of the defensive linemen one man closer to the strength of the formation.

Pick: A pass pattern in which one of the potential receivers hits or screens off a defender, allowing his teammate to be free; also slang for an interception.

Pocket: The area surrounding a passer that is being protected by his blockers.

Point after touchdown (PAT): An extra play allowed after a touchdown in which the team has an opportunity to make one point by kicking the ball through the goalposts or two points by running or passing the ball over the goal line.

Pre-snap read: A cue of defenders' intent evaluated by the quarterback or receivers based on the alignment of the pass defenders.

Prevent defense: A defense sometimes used by a team that is ahead late in a half. It uses extra defensive backs playing deeper than usual and fewer than normal pass rushers.

Primary receiver: The first choice of the passer in a pass pattern.

Punt: A kick made on a scrimmage down that is designed to make the most yardage when possession is changed.

Pursuit: The movement of the defensive players to get them to a spot where they can make the tackle.

Read: Getting an idea of what the opponents are doing by looking at one or more of them as the play develops. It can be done by defenders watching offensive linemen or backs or by passers and receivers watching pass coverage defenders.

Red zone: The area from the 20- to 25-yard line to the goal line. The most critical area for both the offense and the defense.

Rollout: A deep, generally wide path of the quarterback behind the other backs.

Sack: The tackling of the passer before he has a chance to pass.

Safety: A two-point play that occurs when an offensive player is tackled behind his own end zone.

Scramble: The running of the quarterback after he has been forced out of the pocket on a pass play.

Screen: A pass behind the line of scrimmage after a deep drop by the quarterback. Some linemen pull to lead the receiver.

Seams: The areas between the defensive zones, which are more likely to be open to complete passes.

Secondary: The safetymen and cornerbacks.

Shotgun: A formation in which the quarterback sets several yards behind the center to be able to see the field better on a pass play. More wide receivers are also used.

Slot: A back lined up in the area between a split end and the tackle.

Snap: The act of putting the ball in play. It can be handed to the quarterback or thrown (between the legs or to the side) to a back.

Snapper: The offensive lineman who puts the ball in play, usually the center.

Sprint draw: A draw play off of a sprint out move by the quarterback. Also called a "counter trey."

Sprint out: A fast and shallow path of the quarterback.

Streak: A pass pattern in which the receiver runs long and fast.

Strong safety: The safety on the strong side (tight end) of the offense.

Strong side: The side of the offensive line that blocks for the power plays. Usually the side of the tight end is designated the strong side.

Stunt: A defensive maneuver in which linemen create a hole for a backer to move through the line or a movement between defensive linemen that will allow at least one to penetrate the line of scrimmage.

Sweep: A wide offensive power running play.

Tight end: A receiver playing close to the offensive tackle.

Touchback: A play that ends behind the receiver's goal line but in which the impetus of the ball was generated by the other team. There is no score. The ball is moved to the 20-yard line for the first down.

Trap: Blocking of a defensive lineman by an offensive player who did not line up close to him originally. In a trap block the blocker will have his head on the defensive (downfield) side of the opponent, and the play is designed to go inside the block.

Twist: A movement between defensive linemen, especially in a pass situation, in which the linemen cross hoping that at least one will get clear into the backfield.

Two-minute offense or two-minute drill: The attack used by a team late in a half when it is behind and attempting to score while conserving time.

Unbalanced line: An offensive alignment in which four or more linemen are set on one side of the line of scrimmage.

Uprights: The vertical poles that extend up from the crossbar of the goalposts.

Vertical stretch: Forcing the pass defenders to cover deep even if the pass is in the short or intermediate zones.

Waggle: A pass action off a running play in which the quarterback moves wide and deep after faking to a back. Some coaches call it a waggle if the quarterback moves in the direction of the flow behind the backs to whom he has faked. Others call it a waggle if he moves opposite the flow and is protected by a pulling lineman. Most would call this a bootleg.

Walkaway: A position taken by a linebacker or defensive back between a wide receiver and the offensive linemen. It allows the defender to be in position to stop the quick slant pass and still be able to play a wide run.

Wedge: A block in which three or more players block an area.

Wideout: A split end or flanker on the offense, primarily used as a receiver.

Wingback: A back lined up about a yard wider and a yard deeper than the tight end.

X: The split end.

Y: The tight end.

Z: The flanker.

Zone blocking: Two adjacent offensive linemen double-team a down lineman, while both watch the backer. Whichever direction the backer moves, the nearest lineman releases and blocks him. The rule is "four hands on the lineman, four eyes on the backer."

Zone defense: A pass coverage in which the linebackers and defensive backs protect areas and play the ball rather than watch specific men.

Index

Alignments, defensive, 70–71
  in flag and touch football, 160
  secondary, 76–78
Allen, George, 82, 112
Allen, Marcus, 101
American Football Coaches Association, 10, 24, 35, 112
American Football League, 26–27
Appalachian State University, 133–34
Arizona Cardinals, 25
Arizona Wildcats, 132–33
Attack and penetrate defense, 99
Audible, 96, 97, 110
Awards, 24–25

Backfield shift, 54
Backs, 17, 18, 20, 75–76, 149. *See also* Cornerback; Fullback; Halfback; Quarterback; Safety
Balague, Gloria, 33
Ballcarrier, 9, 20, 149, 150, 156, 157
Baltimore Colts, 26, 27
Beamer, Frank, 44–45, 152
Berry, Raymond, 158
Big Ben pass, 142
Big-on-big protection, 63
Big plays, 115–17

Blitz, 14, 74, 116, 119–21, 140, 142
  pickup, 120–21
  planning, 119–20
  strategy for, 96–97
Blocking
  illegal, 128
  of problem defenders, 98
  the punt, 90–91, 151, 152
Boot/bootleg, 62, 63, 126, 143
Boston game, 8
Bowden, Bobby, 37, 129
Brady, Tom, 178, 179
Branch, Cliff, 110
Brigham Young University, 62
Broyles, Frank, 118
Bryant, Paul (Bear), 72, 86
Bull rush, 5
Bump and run, 77, 160
Bunch formation, 12

California Institute of Technology, 169
California Lutheran University, 81, 112
Camp, Walter, 9–10
Carolina Panthers, 117
Carroll, Pete, 23
Carter, Babe, 106
Center, 18

Cheerleading, 29–30
Chicago Bears, 35, 48–49, 101, 110, 112
Chop block, 128
Cleveland Browns, 26
Clip, 21, 156
Clock, 137–44
    at end of game, 140–44
    at end of half, 138–39
    stopping, 21, 137, 155
Closed play, 157
Cloud cover, 14
Club, 5
Coaches/coaching, 33–41
    essentials, 33–34
    salary, 23, 24
    theory, 36–37
    youth football, 34, 165–71
Coaching Football (O'Connor and Flores),
    168, 170
Cochems, Eddie, 12
Coed teams, 28, 154, 157. *See also* Women
    and girls
Collective mentality, 39, 40, 87, 117, 121,
    137, 138
College football, 10, 21, 23–26
College of the Pacific, 12
Columbia University, 8, 9
Conversions, 91–92, 155
Cornerback, 19, 20
Coryell, Don, 62, 108
Counter, 6
Coverage assignments, 84
Cross block, 85
Crossing patterns, 143, 162
Curl, 55

Dallas Cowboys, 44, 54, 110, 117, 181
Deep curl pattern, 65, 66
Defense
    big plays denied by, 116–17
    fantasy football scoring, 176
    in flag and touch football, 159–61
    goal line, 111
    positions in, 19–20
    punt, 88–91
    strategy for, 103–4

    strategy to beat, 97
    tactical adjustments on, 111
    theories of, 69–79
Defensive line theory, 71–74
Delay of game penalties, 128
Denver Broncos, 100
Dietzel, Paul, 130
Dime defense, 76, 110, 111
Ditka, Mike, 110
Dive, 53, 57
Dog/red dog, 14
Donahue, Terry, 148
Dorais, Gus, 12
Double cut, 162
Double reverse, 12
Double slant, 118–19
Double-team, 85
Down, 16, 17
Draft
    in fantasy football, 177–81
    in professional football, 27
Drag, 79
Draw play, 5, 6, 74–75, 98
Drop back pass, 62

Eagle alignment, 71
Eason, Tony, 106
Edwards, Lavelle, 62
Ego involvement, 167
Ellis, William Webb, 7
Elway, John, 138
Empty backfield, 19
Encroachment, 20, 21, 128, 156, 169
Ends, 17–18, 20
Equipment, 22, 154–55

Fair catch, 112
Fake reverse, 85
False pull, 100, 149
Fantasy football, 173–83
    contacting providers, 182–83
    getting into a league, 174
    rules, 175
    schedule, 181–82
    scoring, 175–77
Field, description of, 16

Field goal, 39, 91–92, 144
Field position theory, 43–47
Finesse, 57, 58–60
First down, 115, 154
Five-step drop, 78
Flag and touch football, 28,
    153–63
  defense, 159–61
  offense, 162–63
  rules, 155–57
  scoring, 155
Flag/corner route, 64
Flanker, 17, 18, 55
Flood pattern, 66
Florida State University, 25, 59, 129
Flow, 63
Flying wedge, 9
Football (object)
  control theory, 47
  correct carrying of, 131
  origins of, 7
  positioning of laces, 91
  shape change introduced, 10
Football (sport). *See* College football;
    Fantasy football; Game; High
    school football; Professional
    football; Youth football
Formations, 21, 51–56
Forward pass, 9, 10, 61
Free-kick down, 112
Fringe area, 124
Front, 71
Fullback, 17, 19
Fumbles, 131, 133, 134, 157, 169
Fundamentals, 38–39, 158

Game
  complexity of, 3
  development of theory, 11–16
  history of, 6–10
  length of, 21, 155
  watching, 147–52
Game plan, 4, 102–3
Gap control, 71
Gilman, Sid, 13, 104
Goal area, 124, 143

Goal line, 124, 143, 154
Goal line defense, 111
Goal line offense, 126
Goodall, Roger, 27
Grange, Red (Galloping Ghost),
    13, 54
Green Bay Packers, 48–49, 57
Grogan, Steve, 106
Guard, 15, 18, 148, 149
Gunner, 86, 150, 151

Hail Mary pass, 142
Halfback, 17–18, 19
Hang time, 84, 89, 151
Harvard University, 8, 9, 29
Harvey, Paul, 134
Hash marks, 16
Heffelfinger, Pudge, 26
Heisman Trophy winners, 13, 24
Helmet-related penalties, 128
Hendricks, Ted, 92
High school football, 10, 21, 27–28
Hit and pursue defense, 99
Hit and react technique, 97
Holder, 91, 92
Holding penalty, 128, 130, 149
Hook pattern, 64, 159, 162, 163
Horizontal stretch, 61, 65, 163
Hot receiver, 14, 120

I formation, 58
Illegal procedure, 128
Impact areas, 39–41
Incomplete pass, 10, 25
Influence, 98, 99
Injuries, 4, 7, 8, 22, 100, 139, 178, 182
Intercepted pass, 25

Jersey holding, 149
Johnson, Jimmy, 44, 45
Joseph, Christopher, 25

Kansas City Chiefs, 110
Kansas State University, 130
Keys, 14, 75, 152
Kicker, 91

Kicking game, 150, 170
  coverage assignments, 84
  field goals and conversions, 91–92
  strategy for, 104–5
  tactical adjustments in, 84, 112–13
  theory of, 81–92
Kickoff, 21, 49, 82–85, 112, 157
Kickoff return, 85–86
KISS principle, 168

Landry, Tom, 54
Lateral pass, 9
Leach, Mike, 62
Line of scrimmage, 4, 10, 20–21, 156
Line shift, 54
Linebacker, 20, 74–75
Linemen, 52–53, 149, 151
Lombardi, Vince, 57, 95
Long lateral pass, 85
Long snapper, 170
Loop, 72–73
Los Angeles Rams, 106, 112, 179, 180
Louisiana State University (LSU), 130, 137

MacArthur, Douglas, 25
Man in motion, 12
Man-to-man defense, 55, 65–66, 70, 75, 77,
    79, 97, 103–4, 125, 126, 142
  big plays and, 116, 117
  in flag and touch football, 159, 160–61,
    162
  pass patterns vs., 143
  watching, 148
Manning, Eli, 49
Mastery, 167
McGill University, 8
McKay, John, 58
McMahon, Jim, 106
Miami Dolphins, 101
Michigan State University, 29, 58, 106
Middle guard (Mike), 71
Millan, Matt, 38
Miller, Blake, 179–80
Mismatches, 4, 52, 97
Money generated by football, 23–24

Montana, Joe, 138
Moss, Randy, 179
Most Valuable Player awards, 13, 24
Motion, 54–56

Naismith, James, 11
Namath, Joe, 27
National Association of Intercollegiate
    Athletics (NAIA), 23
National Collegiate Athletic Association
    (NCAA), 9, 23, 155, 156
National Football League (NFL), 10, 26, 27,
    154, 173, 178, 179, 180, 182, 183
Neale, Earl (Greasy), 71
Nelson, Karl, 168
Neutral zone, 20, 156
New England Patriots, 111, 179
New York Giants, 70
New York Jets, 27
Nickel defense, 76, 110, 111
Noseguard/nose tackle, 20, 71
Numbers, jersey, 12, 18
Numbers defense, 72

Oakland Raiders, 62, 92, 100, 101, 108, 110,
    111, 169, 179
O'Connor, Bob, 168
Offense
  fantasy football scoring, 175
  in flag and touch football, 162–63
  formations, 21, 51–56
  goal line, 126
  positions in, 17–19
  red zone, 125
  strategy development for, 96–103
  tactical adjustments on, 109–10
Offset, 19, 20, 116
Ohio State University, 29, 44
O'Leary, George, 45
Olympics, 7, 24
Onside kick, 83, 85, 105
Open play, 157
Option play, 15–16, 59, 63, 70
Out and up pattern, 162
Out pattern, 64–65

Overshift, 72, 99
Overtime, 48–49, 155
Owens, Steve, 70
Owens, Terrell, 106

Pac Ten Defensive Player of the Year
    awards, 25
Partial roll, 62
Pass interference, 128, 160
Pass rush, 5, 157
Passer, 62–64, 131
Passing, 12, 13, 25–26, 47–48, 118–19
    in flag and touch football, 162
    in last two minutes, 141, 142–43
    patterns, 64
    reception drill, 158–59
    strategy for, 101
    theory of, 61–67
Passing tree, 64, 65, 66
Penalties, 21, 127–31, 149
    common, 128
    statistics on, 132–36
Pennsylvania State University, 130
Personal fouls, 128
Peterson, Adrian, 179
Phelan, Jim, 12
Philadelphia Eagles, 71
Pick, 53, 161
Picket, 151, 152
Pierce College, 130
Play-action pass, 62, 74
Playbook, 25, 168
Playing the Offensive Line (Nelson and
    O'Connor), 168
Points, 17, 92, 139. *See also* Scoring
Pop Warner conference, 24, 28
Positions, 17–20
Post, 64
Power play, 51, 57, 60, 143
Practice, 36–37
Pre-snap read, 15
Press coverage, 77, 160
Primary receiver, 142, 143
Princeton University, 8, 9, 28
Professional football, 21, 26–27, 34

Prothro, Tommy, 106
Punt, 36, 86–91, 150–52, 170
    blocking, 90–91, 151, 152
    defense, 88–91
    fake, 87–88
    pooch, 87
    protected, 156
    return, 89–90, 152
Pursuit, 85, 86

Quarterback, 17, 18, 19, 131–32, 148–49
Quickness, 57, 58, 60

Read, 15, 73, 75
Receiver, 66, 148–49
Red zone, 46, 123, 124, 125, 142
Reverse, 85, 100
Rice, Grantland, 171
Robinson, John, 106, 112
Rockne, Knute, 11, 12, 13, 43, 46, 54
Rolle, Myron, 25
Rollout, 62, 63
Roosevelt, Teddy, 7, 9
Rose Bowl, 106, 148
Routes, calling, 64–66
Rowen, Vic, 112
Royal, Darrell, 43, 46, 110
Rugby, 7–8, 9
Rules
    early, 8–10
    for fantasy football, 175
    for flag and touch football, 155–57
    for rugby and soccer, 7–8
    simplified, 16–22
Run and shoot, 142
Running back, 18
Running game, 47–48, 168
    attack options in, 57–60
    strategy for, 99–100
Rutgers University, 8, 28

Sack, 19, 25
Safety (position)
    free, 19, 20, 74, 76
    strong, 19, 20, 74

Safety (scoring), 17
San Diego Chargers, 62, 101, 108
San Francisco 49ers, 26, 35, 62, 168
San Francisco State University, 112
Sanders, Barry, 179
Sanders, Red, 12, 43
Scoring, 17, 123–26
   at end of game, 141–42
   of fantasy football, 175–77
   of flag and touch football, 155
Scramble, 120
Scraping into a gap, 75
Screen pass, 4, 116
Scrimmage down, 112
Seams, 79
Seattle Seahawks, 29, 101
Secondary, 51
Seven-step drop, 78
Shaughnessy, Clark, 13
Shift/shifting, 12, 13, 54–56
Short passes, 67, 103–4, 131–32, 143
Short-yardage (elephant) defense, 111
Shotgun (spread) formation, 12, 13, 19, 59
Shoup, Bob, 81
Sideline pattern, 64–65
Singletary, Mike, 35–36, 165
Sky cover, 14
Slant charge, 72
Slot back, 18, 19
Smith, Dean, 129
Smith, Emmitt, 117
Smith, Steve, 117
Snap, 11, 148, 156
Snapper, 11, 86, 91, 92, 156
Soccer, 7–8
Spacing of the linemen, 52–53
Special teams, 81, 150–52
Split end, 18
Split T attack, 59
Spot pass, 64
Springfield College, 11
Sprint out, 62–63
Squib kick, 82–83
St. Louis University, 12
St. Mary's College, 12

Stagg, Amos Alonzo, 11–12
Stanford University, 13
Statue of liberty play, 12
Stram, Hank, 98
Strategy, 37, 95–108
   defensive, 103–4
   kicking game, 104–5
   offensive, 96–103
Strong side, 72
Stunting, 73–74, 75
Super Bowl, 27, 106, 148, 169, 174, 180, 182
Sweep, 52
Swim move, 5, 150

T formation, 11, 13, 53, 58
Tackle (position), 17, 18, 20
Tackle football, 28, 153, 156, 168
Tactical adjustments, 37, 84, 109–13
Tailback, 17, 19, 100
Tampa Bay Buccaneers, 169
Teamwork, 35, 37
Televised games, 21, 24
Ten-yard out pattern, 162
Texas Tech University, 62
Third downs, 115, 118
Thorpe, Jim, 26
Three-step drop, 78
Throwback area, opening in, 115
Tight end, 14, 17
Tillman, Pat, 25
Time-outs, 21, 138, 139, 140, 141, 142
Title IX, 23
Touch football. *See* Flag and touch football
Touchback, 10
Touchdown, 17, 44–47, 139, 142, 180
Trap, 53, 85
Tressel, Jim, 44
Triple option, 59
Try, 7
Turnovers
   causes and prevention, 131–32
   statistics on, 132–36
Twist, 99
Two-minute offense/drill, 40, 137, 138,
   141–43

Umbrella defense, 70
Unbalanced line, 54
Undershift, 99
Unitas, Johnny, 158
University of Alabama, 72, 137
University of Arkansas, 49, 118
University of California at Davis, 29
University of California at Los Angeles
    (UCLA), 12, 25, 29, 106, 148, 169
University of Central Florida, 45
University of Chicago, 11
University of Idaho, 12
University of Mississippi, 49
University of Notre Dame, 11, 12, 13
University of Southern California (USC),
    23, 29, 58
Unsportsmanlike conduct, 128
Uprights, 113

Valley College, 129–30
Vermeil, Dick, 82
Vertical stretch, 61, 65, 163
Virginia Polytechnic Institute and
    University (Virginia Tech), 44, 135, 152

Waggle, 62, 63
Waivers, 181
Wake Forest University, 133–36
Walsh, Bill, 13, 62, 111, 168
Warner, Kurt, 180
Warner, Pop, 13
Washington State Cougars, 132–33

Wave, 29
Weather, 46, 47–48
Weber State University, 137
Wedge, 85, 86, 150
Weller, Rob, 29
West Coast offense, 62
Wide countering (reverse) area, opening
    in, 115
Wide receiver, 18, 19, 111
Wideout, 17, 18
Wing formation, 12, 13
Wingback, 18
Winning, 34, 165, 167, 171
    impact areas, 39–41
    theories of, 43–49
Women and girls, 23–24, 27, 28, 153, 155.
    See also Coed teams

Yale University, 8, 9, 11, 29
Yost, Fielding, 106
Youth football, 34, 154, 165–71
    motivation in, 166–67
    overview of, 27–28
    theory of, 168–71

Zone blocking, 15, 16, 64
Zone coverage, 78–79, 117
Zone defense, 55, 66, 75, 76, 97, 103–4, 143
    in flag and touch football, 159, 160, 161,
        162, 163
    in youth football, 169
Zuppke, Bob, 54

About the Authors

◆◆

Bob O'Connor has coached at every level of football, from junior high through high school and university, and with two Super Bowl coaches. He has coached not only in the United States but also in Europe and Oceania. He is one of the longest-standing members of the American Football Coaches Association. His depth and breadth of experience gives him a comprehensive knowledge of the game that he can impart to you.

Tom Flores was the first man to win four Super Bowl rings and is one of only two who have won rings as both a player and coach—having coached the Raiders to two Super Bowl titles. He still owns the Raiders record for most touchdown passes in a game at seven. His retirement from coaching brought him to the broadcast booth, where he now delights the fans with his rare insights into the game. He and Bob have written several books for coaches, but he felt the need to write one for non-coaches who might be "utterly confused."